# SATURN
## AND BEYOND

To the memory of
*John and Rae Jeppson,*
whose daughter I was fortunate enough to marry.

# SATURN
## AND BEYOND

## ISAAC ASIMOV

Diagrams by Giulio Maestro

Lothrop, Lee & Shepard Company
*A Division of William Morrow & Co., Inc.* • *New York*

Lothrop Books on Astronomy by

ISAAC ASIMOV

JUPITER, THE LARGEST PLANET
ALPHA CENTAURI, THE NEAREST STAR
MARS, THE RED PLANET
SATURN AND BEYOND

*Title page photograph:* NASA
*Frontispiece:* Mount Wilson and Palomar Observatories

First Edition
1   2   3   4   5   6   7   8   9   10

Library of Congress Cataloging in Publication Data

Asimov, Isaac (date)
   Saturn and beyond.

   SUMMARY: Presents a detailed discussion of the four outermost planets in our solar system.
   1.  Saturn (Planet)—Juvenile literature.  2.  Uranus (Planet)—Juvenile literature.  3.  Neptune (Planet)—Juvenile literature.  4.  Pluto (Planet)—Juvenile literature.
   [1.  Planets.  2.  Solar system]  I.  Maestro, Giulio.  II.  Title.
   QB671.A84       523.4       78-21996
   ISBN 0-688-41876-7
   ISBN 0-688-51876-1 lib. bdg.

# CONTENTS

1 · THE ORIGINAL SOLAR SYSTEM     15

*The Planets · The Slow Planet · The Distant Planet ·
Distance in Kilometers · The Shape of the Solar System*


2 · SATURN     39

*Brightness of the Sun · Brightness of the Planets ·
The Spinning of the Planets · The Axial Tipping of the Planets*


3 · THE RINGS OF SATURN     59

*The Discovery of the Rings · The Size of the Rings ·
The Makeup of the Rings · The Origin of the Rings*


4 · TITAN     74

*Mass and Density · The Structure of Planets ·
Surface Gravity · The Size of the Satellites ·
Titan's Atmosphere*

5 · THE SATELLITES OF SATURN    101

*The Discovery of Saturn's Satellites · The Orbits of
Saturn's Satellites · The Skies of Saturn's Satellites · The Size of
Saturn's Satellites*

6 · COMETS AND ASTEROIDS    133

*Halley's Comet and Others · From Icarus to Hidalgo ·
Chiron*

7 · URANUS    151

*The Discovery of Uranus · The Properties of Uranus ·
The Satellites of Uranus · The Rings of Uranus*

8 · NEPTUNE    173

*The Discovery of Neptune · The Outer Planets ·
Triton · Nereid*

9 · PLUTO    195

*The Discovery of Pluto · The Orbit of Pluto ·
The Size of Pluto*

GLOSSARY    209

INDEX    217

# LIST
# OF
# TABLES

1 · Period of Revolution of the Six Planets     17

2 · Orbital Eccentricity of the Six Planets     25

3 · Relative Distance of the Six Planets from the Sun     25

4 · Perihelia and Aphelia of the Six Planets     27

5 · Distance of the Six Planets from the Sun     30

6 · Saturn at Perihelion and Aphelion     31

7 · Average Orbital Velocity of the Six Planets     34

8 · Inclination to the Ecliptic of the Six Planets     36

9 · Distance from the Ecliptic for the Six Planets     37

10 · Apparent Width of the Sun Seen from the
Six Planets     40

11 · Sun's Area and Radiation from the Six Planets     42

12 · Apparent Brightness of the Six Planets     45

13 · Apparent Width of the Six Planets     46

14 · Diameter of the Six Planets     47

15 · Albedos of the Six Planets     49

16 · Rotation Periods of the Six Planets     53

17 · Equatorial Speeds of the Six Planets     54

18 · Polar Diameters of the Six Planets     55

19 · Oblateness of the Six Planets     56

20 · Axial Tipping of the Six Planets     58

21 · Saturn's Ring System     66

22 · Width of Saturn's Rings     67

23 · Area of Saturn's Rings     67

24 · Radius and Roche Limit of the Six Planets     73

25 · Masses of the Six Planets     77

26 · Densities of the Six Planets     78

27 · Abundance of the Elements     80

28 · Substances Making up the Solar System     82

29 · Surface Gravity of the Six Planets     86

30 · Escape Velocity from the Six Planets     88

31 · Apparent Brightness of the Six Satellites     89

32 · Diameters of the Six Satellites     90

33 · Volumes of the Six Satellites     91

34 · Volumes of the Six Satellites Relative to
     Their Planets     92

35 · Masses of the Six Satellites     94

36 · Densities of the Six Satellites     94

37 · Surface Gravity of the Six Satellites     96

38 · Escape Velocity from the Six Satellites     96

39 · Size of the Six Satellites as Seen from
     Their Planets     97

40 · Satellites of Saturn     105

41 · Distance of Saturn's Satellites     106

42 · Period of Revolution of Saturn's Satellites     110

43 · Orbital Eccentricity of Saturn's Satellites     112

44 · Orbital Inclination of Saturn's Satellites     116

45 · Size of Saturn as Seen from Its Satellites     118

46 · Brightness of Saturn's Satellites     125

47 · Diameters of Saturn's Satellites     126

48 · Apparent Diameters of Saturn's Satellites     127

49 · Masses of Saturn's Satellites     129

50 · Surface Gravity of Saturn's Satellites     130

51 · Cassini's Division     130

52 · Densities of Saturn's Satellites     132

53 · Brightness of Uranus    155

54 · Apparent Motion of Uranus    156

55 · Apparent Size of Uranus    156

56 · Period of Revolution and Distance of the
Satellites of Uranus    164

57 · Diameter and Mass of the Satellites of Uranus    166

58 · Apparent Diameter of Satellites of Uranus as Seen
in Uranus's Sky    167

59 · Size of Uranus as Seen from Its Satellites    168

60 · The Titius-Bode Law    176

61 · Distance of the Outer Planets    180

62 · Orbits of the Outer Planets    182

63 · Diameters of the Outer Planets    183

64 · Rotation of the Outer Planets    185

65 · Masses of the Large Satellites    187

66 · Masses of the Outer Planets    187

67 · Densities of the Outer Planets    188

68 · Gravitational Pull of the Outer Planets    188

# LIST
# OF
# FIGURES

1 · Circle and Ellipse    23
2 · Different Ellipses    23
3 · Perihelion and Aphelion    26
4 · The Original Solar System    32
5 · Angles    36
6 · Relative Size of the Six Planets    48
7 · Axial Tipping and Revolution    57
8 · Saturn's Rings as Seen from Earth    63
9 · Saturn and Its Rings    65
10 · The Orbits of Saturn's Inner Satellites    107
11 · The Orbits of Saturn's Middle Satellites    108
12 · The Orbit of Saturn's Outer Satellite    109
13 · Saturn and Phoebe    113
14 · Orbital Inclinations    115
15 · Phoebe the Retrograde Satellite    117
16 · Halley's Comet    136
17 · The Trojan Asteroids    144
18 · Hidalgo    146
19 · Chiron    149
20 · The Orbit of Uranus    158
21 · The Axial Tilt of Uranus    160
22 · The Satellites of Uranus    165

23 · The Rings of Uranus    171
24 · The Orbit of Neptune    181
25 · Relative Size of the Outer Planets    184
26 · Triton    190
27 · Nereid    192
28 · The Orbit of Pluto    202
29 · Neptune and Pluto    203

# 1

## THE
## ORIGINAL
## SOLAR
## SYSTEM

### *The Planets*

When human beings first began to look at the sky with attention, they noticed that it was filled with stars on clear nights.
The stars seemed to exist in a fixed pattern that stayed the
same from night to night.

The whole sky, with the stars, seemed to change position
slowly and regularly when viewed at some fixed time each night
—say, soon after sunset. The whole vault of the sky seemed to
turn, and it took a whole year for it to make a complete turn
and come back to its original position. The stars held to their
pattern, however, as the sky turned.

There were seven objects in the sky, though, that changed
position against the background of the "fixed stars."

One of these is the sun, a circle of brilliant light, which is
by far the brightest object in the sky. When it is in the sky, it
drowns out all the stars with its light. What's more, scattered
sunlight turns the sky blue.

Just after the sun sets and just before it rises, you can see
the pattern of the stars near it. From the way the pattern shifts,
it is clear that the sun moves against that pattern from day
to day.

Then there is the moon. Like the sun, it is a circle of light, but one that is far dimmer. The stars can be seen when it is shining in the sky, so that the way in which it shifts position against the pattern of the stars, from night to night, is easy to work out.

The moon moves through the sky at a rate that is far greater than that of the sun. This means it changes position with respect to the sun. On occasion, it is close to the sun and sometimes can be seen to shine very faintly in the daytime when sunlight doesn't quite drown it out. Sometimes, on the other hand, it is far from the sun and shines high in the sky after the sun has set. Then it can seem quite bright.

The moon shines only because it reflects light reaching it from the sun. Different parts of it receive sunlight at different times, depending on how far it is in the sky from the sun. That is why the moon seems to change shape. Sometimes we see it as a perfectly round circle of light, sometimes as a semicircle, sometimes as a crescent.

In addition to the sun and the moon, there are five more objects in the sky that move against the background of the fixed stars, each at its own speed and in its own fashion. These five look like stars but shine more brightly than the other stars do.

Two of these starlike objects, in the course of their changing position, never move very far from the sun, so that we only see them in the evening sky for a period of time after the sun has set, or in the sky of dawn for a period of time before the sun rises. These objects are Mercury and Venus.

Because Mercury and Venus are always near the sun, we never see them in the sky at midnight when the sun is shining down on the opposite side of the Earth. Mercury and Venus are then near the sun, as usual, and are shining down on the opposite side of the Earth, too.

That leaves three bright starlike objects that can shine at any distance from the sun and can therefore, in the course of their motions, be in the sky at any time of the night, even at midnight. We call these objects Mars, Jupiter, and Saturn.

The ancient Greeks called these objects that moved, or wandered, against the background of the fixed stars *planetes*. That means "wanderers" in Greek, and the word has come down to us as "planets."

The ancients counted seven planets: the sun, the moon, Mercury, Venus, Mars, Jupiter, and Saturn. They felt that these planets all revolved about the Earth, which they considered to be the center of the universe.

In 1543, however, a Polish astronomer, Nicolaus Copernicus (koh-PUR-nih-kus, 1473–1543) published a book which showed that it made more sense to suppose that the various starlike planets—Mercury, Venus, Mars, Jupiter, and Saturn—all revolved around the sun, and that only the moon revolved around the Earth. What's more, the Earth, with the moon tagging along, also revolved around the sun.

This new theory was slowly accepted by astronomers, and their view of what a planet might be changed. They decided

# TABLE 1

## Period of Revolution of the Six Planets

| | PERIOD OF REVOLUTION | |
|---|---|---|
| PLANET | DAYS | YEARS |
| Mercury | 88.0 | 0.241 |
| Venus | 224.7 | 0.615 |
| Earth | 365.25 | 1.000 |
| Mars | 687.0 | 1.881 |
| Jupiter | 4,332.5 | 11.862 |
| **Saturn** | **10,759.3** | **29.458** |

that a planet was any body that revolved about the sun. The sun did not revolve about itself, of course, so it was no longer viewed as a planet. Nor was the moon, which revolved around the Earth rather than around the sun.

That left Mercury, Venus, Mars, Jupiter, and Saturn as planets and to them was added Earth itself as another planet.

The sun and these six planets, plus Earth's attendant moon, came to be called the "solar system" from the Latin word *sol*, which means "sun." After all, it is the sun which is the center and, it would seem, the ruler of the planets, so it seemed only right that the system should be named for it.

### The Slow Planet

The solar system, as it was known to Copernicus, consisted, then, of exactly eight bodies and no more: the sun, the six planets, and the moon. We can call that the original solar system, but, as we shall see, there is much more to the solar system as we now know it than just those eight bodies.

The planet that is nearest the sun is Mercury. Then, moving outward, we have in order: Venus, Earth (plus the moon), Mars, Jupiter, and Saturn.

How can we tell that that's the order?

If we just look at the sky, we can't tell whether any particular object is farther than any other. However, if we look at the sky night after night, and watch how each planet moves among the stars, we see that each moves at a different speed. If we mark the position of each compared to that of the sun, we see that some planets make a complete circle about the sun more rapidly than others do.

The time for a complete circle about the sun is called the "period of revolution." The periods of revolution for the six planets of the original solar system are given in Table 1.

It seems natural to suppose that the longer it takes a planet to circle the sun, the longer the path it is taking and the farther it must therefore be from the sun.

Since Saturn takes thirty years to complete its revolution about the sun, two and a half times as long as Jupiter takes and sixteen times as long as Mars takes, it seems natural to suppose that it must be the most distant of the planets.

This very slowness of Saturn gave it its name.

The Greeks named the planets after various gods of theirs, and tried to pick suitable gods for each planet.

For instance, the planet which moves across the sky most quickly was named by them Hermes (HUR'meez) who was the wing-footed messenger of the gods. The Romans did not keep the Greek names, however, but used the names of their own gods, trying to choose those they considered to be the equivalent of the Greek gods. The Romans had a god named Mercurius, for instance, who was their god of trade. The Romans felt he corresponded to the Greek Hermes, so they named the innermost planet Mercurius. We have kept the Roman names, though we sometimes make small changes, and in English, the name of the innermost planet is Mercury.

The second planet is at times brighter than any of the rest of them and sometimes shines in the evening sky like a beautiful jewel. The Greeks therefore named it Aphrodite (AF-roh-DIGH-tee) after their goddess of love and beauty. The Romans used their goddess of love and beauty instead and called it Venus.

The third planet is Earth.

The fourth planet has a distinctly reddish gleam to it and the Greeks associated it with blood and war. They named it for their war-god, Ares (AY-reez), and the Romans changed that to their war-god, Mars.

The fifth planet is the brightest except for Venus. In the midnight sky, the sun and Venus are always absent. If the fifth planet is then high in the sky and if the moon is not present, the fifth planet is the brightest object in the sky. What's more, while Venus changes brightness according to its position relative to the sun, the fifth planet stays rather steadily bright whatever its position in the night sky.

The Greeks named it for the ruler of the gods, therefore, Zeus (zyoos) and the Romans used the name of their chief god, Jupiter.

That left the sixth planet. It moved so slowly, so much more slowly than any of the others, that the Greeks thought it fitting to name it for some old, old god, one who might be expected to move slowly out of old age.

As it happens, Zeus had not always been the ruler of the gods, according to the Greek myths. Before he existed, it was his father, Kronos, who ruled the gods and the universe. Eventually, Zeus warred on his father, overthrew him, and ruled in his place. Kronos lived on after that, but in retirement, and the Greeks always pictured him as an old man.

They named the sixth planet, therefore, which moves the most slowly, Kronos (KROH-nus).

The Romans didn't have any myth like this. They did, however, have a god named Saturnus, who was their god of agriculture. Among the Greeks, there were some who considered Kronos a god of agriculture. The Romans therefore identified Saturnus with Kronos and named the sixth planet Saturnus, and we therefore call it Saturn.

The ancients, who counted seven planets, also knew of seven metals: gold, silver, copper, mercury, iron, tin, and lead.

It seemed natural to them to suppose that each of the seven metals corresponded to one or another of the seven planets. Surely gold must represent the sun, and silver the moon. Copper, which was the third most rare and beautiful, would then be Venus, the brightest object after the sun and moon.

Mercury, the quick-moving liquid metal, was associated with the quick-moving planet of the same name. Iron, the metal used for war weapons, was associated with Mars, and tin, a white metal, was associated with the white-gleaming Jupiter.

That left lead for Saturn and that seemed a very good choice. Lead is heavy, dull and gray. It seemed to symbolized the heaviness, dullness and grayness of old age and therefore fit the slow steps of aged Kronos.

We still associate lead and Saturn today. A combination of lead and oxygen, for instance, is a deep red in color, and an old name for it is "saturnine red."

"Saturnine colic" is also an old medical term for lead poisoning. Then, too, people who are of a heavy and gloomy disposition are sometimes said to be "saturnine" because they are thought to be under the leaden influence of the planet Saturn.

Another group of seven are the days of the week, and in ancient times each was associated with one of the planets. The seventh day was associated with Saturn and we still call it "Saturday" in English.

### The Distant Planet

The ancients thought that the planets traveled about the Earth in perfect circles. While Copernicus realized the planets traveled about the sun and not about the Earth, he clung to the notion of perfect circles. To this day, we call the path taken by any astronomical body around any other an "orbit," from a Latin word meaning "circle."

The actual path taken by the planets across the sky did not, however, seem to fit what would be expected of a circle. The Greek astronomers worked out complicated systems to account for that.

The complications finally ended in 1609, when a German astronomer, Johannes Kepler (1571–1630), was able to show that the orbits of the planets were not circles at all, but ellipses.

An ellipse looks like a flattened circle that is exactly alike on both ends. In a circle, any line passing through the center is a diameter, and all the diameters of a particular circle are equal in length. In an ellipse, the diameters are of different lengths (see Figure 1).

The longest diameter of an ellipse runs from one narrow end to the other and is called the "major axis." The diameter that is the shortest is the "minor axis." The two axes cross at right angles (that is, if one goes horizontally, the other goes vertically). Where the two axes cross is the center of the ellipse.

On the major axis of the ellipse are located two points called "foci"; each one of them is a "focus."

The foci are on opposite sides of the center and at equal distances from it. The foci are located in such a way that if a straight line is drawn from one focus to any point on the ellipse and from that point to the other focus, the sum of the lengths of the two straight lines is always equal to the length of the major axis.

The more flattened an ellipse is, the farther the foci are from the center and the closer they are to the ends (see Figure 2).

The distance of the foci from the center is the measure of the "eccentricity" of the ellipse. The term comes from Greek words meaning "away from the center."

If the foci are only $\frac{1}{100}$ of the way from the center to the end of the ellipse, the eccentricity is 0.01. With such a small eccentricity, you can't notice the flattening. Such an ellipse looks so much like a circle, you can't tell the difference without making careful measurements. (For a circle, the foci are exactly at the center and the eccentricity is 0.)

If the foci are halfway from the center to the ends, the eccentricity is 0.5 and the ellipse looks like an egg that has the same curve on both sides. If the foci are nine tenths of the way from the center to the end, the eccentricity is 0.9 and the ellipse looks rather like a cigar.

Once astronomers realized that the planetary orbits were

## Fig. 1—Circle and Ellipse

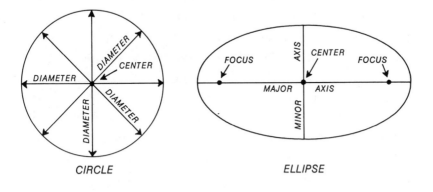

CIRCLE                    ELLIPSE

## Fig. 2—Different Ellipses

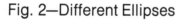
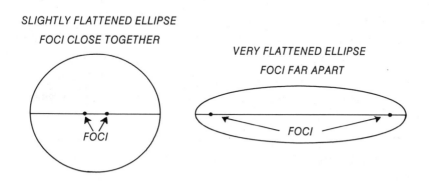

ellipses, they could calculate their shapes from the changing positions of each planet in the sky, and work out the eccentricities of each one. The results are given in Table 2.

None of these eccentricities is high. Mercury's orbit, if you were to draw it on paper, might look a little bit flattened but all the rest would look just like circles to the eye. It is because they are so close to being circles that the ancient astronomers thought they were. If the elliptical orbits had had really high eccentricities, astronomers would have seen at once that circles were out of the question as a way of describing the orbit.

When Kepler first worked out the elliptical orbits of the planets, he couldn't tell how large they were in the units used for measuring distance on Earth. He couldn't tell their "absolute size" in other words. He could, however, tell that one orbit might be twice as large as another or 3.4 times as large. He could work out the "relative size."

Suppose, for instance, that we consider the distance from the Earth to the sun to be equal to 1 and call that distance "1 astronomical unit" or, in abbreviation, "1 A.U." All the other distances can be compared to Earth's and all can be given in A.U. This is done in Table 3, where you can see that Saturn is nearly ten times as far from the sun as Earth is.

If planetary orbits were circles and if the sun were located at the center, then the distance of the planet from the sun would remain the same at every point in the orbit. However, the orbits are ellipses and Kepler showed that the sun was not at the center of the ellipse but at one focus.

When the sun is at one focus of the ellipse, that means the sun is nearer one end of the ellipse than the other (see Figure 3). When the planet, as it moves in its orbit, passes the end of the major axis that is on the side of the focus that holds the sun, it is nearer the sun than when it is at any other point in the orbit. That nearest point is the "perihelion" from Greek words meaning "near the sun."

# TABLE 2

## Orbital Eccentricity of the Six Planets

| PLANET | ORBITAL ECCENTRICITY |
|--------|----------------------|
| Mercury | 0.2056 |
| Venus | 0.0068 |
| Earth | 0.0167 |
| Mars | 0.0934 |
| Jupiter | 0.0485 |
| **Saturn** | **0.0556** |

# TABLE 3

## Relative Distance of the Six Planets from the Sun

| PLANET | DISTANCE FROM THE SUN (A.U.) |
|--------|------------------------------|
| Mercury | 0.387 |
| Venus | 0.723 |
| Earth | 1.000 |
| Mars | 1.524 |
| Jupiter | 5.203 |
| **Saturn** | **9.539** |

Fig. 3—Perihelion and Aphelion

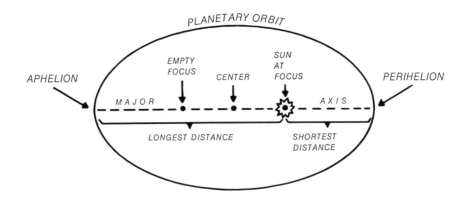

As it leaves the perihelion, the planet moves farther and farther from the sun, until it reaches the other end of the major axis, when it is farther from the sun than at any other point in the orbit. That point is the "aphelion" from Greek words meaning "away from the sun."

The greater the eccentricity of a planetary orbit, the greater the difference in the distance of the planet from the sun at perihelion and aphelion. Because the eccentricities of the planetary ellipses are so small, the difference in distance isn't great among the six planets, except for Mercury (see Table 4).

As you can see, when Saturn is at perihelion and Earth is at aphelion, Saturn is 8.86 times as far from the sun as Earth is. When Saturn is at aphelion and Earth is at perihelion, Saturn is 10.24 times as far from the sun as Earth is.

# TABLE 4

## Perihelia and Aphelia of the Six Planets

| PLANET | DISTANCE AT PERIHELION (A.U.) | DISTANCE AT APHELION (A.U.) | DIFFERENCE IN TWO DISTANCES (PERCENT) |
|---|---|---|---|
| Mercury | 0.308 | 0.467 | 51.6 |
| Venus | 0.719 | 0.729 | 1.4 |
| Earth | 0.984 | 1.017 | 3.4 |
| Mars | 1.381 | 1.666 | 20.6 |
| Jupiter | 4.951 | 5.455 | 10.2 |
| **Saturn** | **9.008** | **10.069** | **11.8** |

## *Distance in Kilometers*

But how far away is Saturn from the sun in actual earthly units?

If we knew how far the Earth was from the sun in earthly units, then we'd be able to calculate all the other planetary distances. If we knew how far any planet was from any other at some particular time, we could calculate all the other planetary positions.

In Kepler's time, the only way of judging the distance of a heavenly body was to make use of "parallax" (from Greek words meaning "change of position").

You can see how this works if you hold a finger in front of your eyes at arm's length. If you close one eye, you will see the finger against some object in the background. If you hold your finger and your head steady and close the other eye, you will see a change in the apparent position of your finger against the background. The change in position is the parallax.

If you bring the finger closer to yourself you will see that the change in position, as you use first one eye and then the other, becomes greater. By measuring the parallax, you can determine the distance of your finger from your eye.

By using your eyes only, you cannot measure very great distances. For objects across the street, the parallax becomes too small to measure accurately, Fortunately, the shift depends not only on distance but on the separation of the two points from which the object is viewed. Your eyes are separated by only a small distance that is not much of a "base line." You could use a larger one.

You could plant two stakes a block apart. If you viewed an object first from one stake, then from the other, you would increase the amount of parallax for a given distance, and an object could then be much farther away before the parallax became too small to measure. And your base line might be longer still, even much longer.

Suppose you observed the moon at a particular time from a particular position on Earth's surface. At the same time, someone else could observe it from another nation. The first observer would see it at a certain distance from a nearby star; the second observer would see it at a slightly different distance from that same star. From the shift of position and from a knowledge of how far apart the two observation points are, the distance of the moon can be calculated.

This can be done. By Kepler's time it was known how far away the moon is. The best current figure is that the moon's average distance from the Earth is 384,390 kilometers * (238,-860 miles). Since the moon travels in an elliptical orbit about the Earth, with the Earth at one focus, it is sometimes a little closer than that and sometimes a little farther.

The Earth's equator has a total length of 40,070 kilometers (24,900 miles). This means that the distance of the Earth to

---

* In the United States, the common unit for measuring distance is the "mile." In the rest of the world, the "kilometer" is used. Scientists, even in the United States, use kilometers. A kilometer is just about ⅝ of a mile.

the moon is only 9.6 times as long as a trip around the equator. This is not really very much and these days many human beings travel, in a lifetime, a distance far greater than the distance to the moon.

The moon, however, is the closest astronomical body to the Earth. The other planets are much farther away. How much farther?

Unfortunately, the moon's parallax does not help us here since the moon is not included in the relative scale of the solar system worked out by Kepler. We need the parallax of a planet, but the planets are so far away that their parallaxes are too small to measure by eye alone no matter how long you make the base line on Earth.

In 1609, however, the Italian scientist Galileo (gahl-ih-LAY-oh, 1564–1642) constructed a crude telescope and pointed it at the heavens. It magnified objects and made it possible to measure small movements that were not large enough to measure by the unaided eye. With the years, telescopes improved.

In 1670 the Italian-French astronomer Giovanni Domenico Cassini (ka-SEE-nee, 1625–1712) observed the position of Mars from his observatory in Paris. At the same time another French astronomer, Jean Richer (ree-SHAY, 1630–1696), observed the position of Mars from French Guiana, thousands of kilometers away. The change in the position of Mars against nearby stars was tiny, but with the telescope it could be measured.

Cassini could calculate the distance of Mars from Earth at that particular time, and from that he could calculate all the other planetary distances in the solar system, including especially the distance of the Earth from the sun.

Cassini's values were a little low, but they have been improved since and we now know that the average distance of the Earth from the sun, the Astronomical Unit, is 149,597,870 kilometers (92,960,116 miles).

When we come to distances in the millions of kilometers,

that becomes difficult to grasp. Suppose we consider light, however.

Light moves through vacuum at a speed of 299,792.4562 kilometers per second (186,282.3959 miles per second). That is as fast as anything in this universe can possibly travel, and scientists are quite convinced that it is impossible, even in theory, for ordinary objects to move faster than light.

If a beam of light could be made to go around the Earth at the equator, it would make one complete turn about the Earth in just under one seventh of a second, and it would travel from the Earth to the moon in just 1.28 seconds. That is an indication of how incredibly fast light is.

If we know, then, the exact length of the Astronomical Unit, we can calculate the distance of each planet from the sun in kilometers, or in miles, or in the length of time it would take light to travel the distance. This is done in Table 5.

# TABLE 5

## Distance of the Six Planets from the Sun

| PLANET | AVERAGE DISTANCE FROM THE SUN | | TIME FOR LIGHT TO TRAVEL FROM SUN TO PLANET (MINUTES) |
|---|---|---|---|
| | KILOMETERS | MILES | |
| Mercury | 57,900,000 | 35,800,000 | 3.2 |
| Venus | 108,200,000 | 67,200,000 | 6.0 |
| Earth | 149,600,000 | 93,000,000 | 8.3 |
| Mars | 227,900,000 | 141,600,000 | 12.7 |
| Jupiter | 778,300,000 | 483,600,000 | 43.2 |
| **Saturn** | **1,427,000,000** | **886,700,000** | **79.3** |

Now we have an idea of how enormous the solar system is and how far away Saturn is. Of the six planets known in the times of Galileo and Cassini, Saturn, the farthest, was nearly one and a half billion kilometers from the sun. So enormous is the distance of Saturn that light speeding from the sun at an incredible velocity nevertheless takes well over an hour to reach Saturn. If Saturn were to vanish from its position in the sky while we were looking at it, we wouldn't be aware of the disappearance for 79.3 minutes, for that's how long it would take for the last bit of light the planet had reflected before it disappeared to reach us.

Mercury, Venus, Earth, and Mars are all within 250 million kilometers (150 million miles) of the sun. They make up the "inner solar system." Outside, though, are Jupiter, sailing through space 550 million kilometers (340 million miles) beyond Mars, and Saturn, which is 650 million kilometers (400 million miles) beyond Jupiter.

If we were to try to draw a map of the planetary orbits in accurate scale, the inner solar system would be crowded in near the sun, and Jupiter and Saturn would seem at lonely distances indeed (see Figure 4).

Of course, Saturn isn't always at its average distance from the sun. It is considerably closer at perihelion and farther at aphelion (see Table 6).

# TABLE 6

## Saturn at Perihelion and Aphelion

| SATURN | DISTANCE FROM THE SUN | | TIME FOR LIGHT TO TRAVEL FROM SUN TO SATURN (MINUTES) |
| | KILOMETERS | MILES | |
| --- | --- | --- | --- |
| At Perihelion | 1,348,000,000 | 837,600,000 | 74.9 |
| At Aphelion | 1,508,000,000 | 937,000,000 | 83.8 |

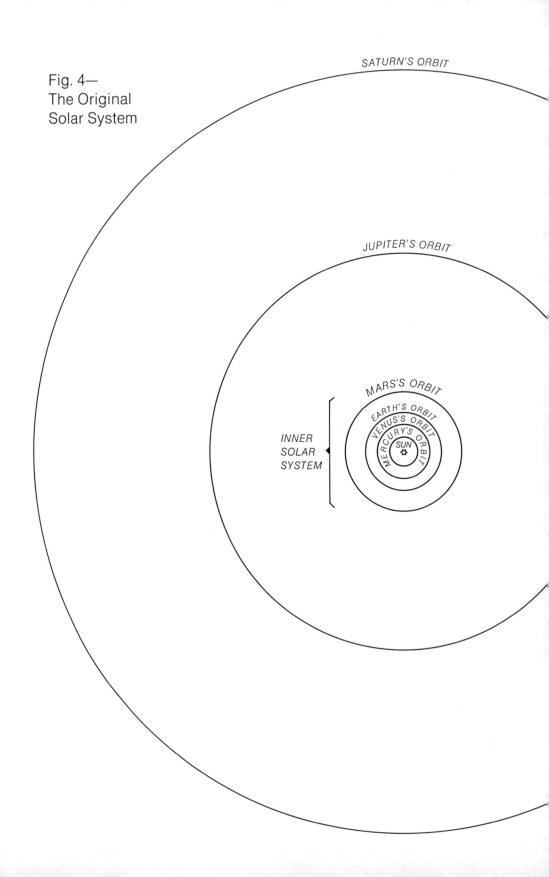

Fig. 4—
The Original
Solar System

SATURN'S ORBIT

JUPITER'S ORBIT

MARS'S ORBIT

EARTH'S ORBIT

VENUS'S ORBIT

MERCURY'S ORBIT

SUN

INNER
SOLAR
SYSTEM

At aphelion, Saturn is 160,000,000 kilometers (100,000,000 miles) farther from the sun than at perihelion. This is a large difference equal to the whole distance of the Earth from the sun. So enormous is the distance of Saturn from the sun, however, that a difference in distance equal only to the distance of Earth from the sun is hardly noticeable.

How far is Saturn from the Earth?

When Earth and Saturn happen to be on the same side of the sun as each travels along its orbit, Saturn is closer to the Earth than it is to the sun. If the two planets are on opposite sides of the sun, then Saturn is farther from the Earth than it is from the sun.

Suppose Saturn is at its perihelion and the Earth is on the same side of the sun as Saturn is. Saturn is then as close to Earth as it ever gets. It is only 1,200,000,000 kilometers (745,-000,000 miles) from Earth. If Saturn is at its aphelion and the Earth is on the opposite side of the sun, then Saturn is as far away from the Earth as it ever gets. It is then 1,658,000,000 kilometers (1,030,000,000 miles) away.

Saturn, in making one revolution about the sun, travels along an orbital path that is nearly 9,000,000,000 kilometers (5,600,-000,000 miles) long. This is nearly ten times as long as the path followed by the Earth in its revolution about the sun.

Since Saturn's path is nearly ten times as long as Earth's, it wouldn't be surprising if it took Saturn nearly ten times as long to make one revolution about the sun as it takes Earth. Actually, it takes Saturn not quite thirty times as long to do so. Why is that?

In 1687 the English scientist Isaac Newton (1642–1727) worked out the theory of universal gravitation, and showed that the planets circled the sun because they were under the influence of the sun's gravitational attraction.

Newton showed that the gravitational influence of any body weakens with distance. Therefore a distant planet, under a weaker influence, would whip around the sun more slowly than a nearby planet would. And, as a matter of fact, when the orbital speed of a planet is calculated (from its apparent motion across the sky and its known distance) it does turn out that the farther it is from the sun, the more slowly it moves in its orbit (see Table 7).

## TABLE 7

### Average Orbital Velocity of the Six Planets

| | AVERAGE ORBITAL VELOCITY | |
|---|---|---|
| PLANET | KILOMETERS PER SECOND | MILES PER SECOND |
| Mercury | 47.89 | 29.76 |
| Venus | 35.03 | 21.77 |
| Earth | 29.79 | 18.51 |
| Mars | 24.13 | 14.99 |
| Jupiter | 13.06 | 8.52 |
| **Saturn** | **9.64** | **5.99** |

Not only is Saturn's path around the sun nearly ten times longer than Earth's is, but Saturn moves only one third as quickly. No wonder it takes Saturn thirty times as long to go around the sun as it takes Earth.

### The Shape of the Solar System

Suppose we imagine a piece of paper, absolutely flat and very, very thin. This would be like something mathematicians call a "plane," from a Latin word meaning "flat."

Imagine a plane extending through the solar system and

passing through the center of the sun and through the ellipse that represents Earth's orbit. The Earth as it moved around the sun would remain in this plane at all times.

The plane of the Earth's orbit is called the "ecliptic." The reason for this is that eclipses of the sun or moon take place only when the moon, in its orbit, passes through the ecliptic, because only then can it pass between Earth and the sun to eclipse the latter, or directly behind the Earth so as to get into its shadow and be eclipsed itself.

Imagine the plane of the ecliptic spread throughout the solar system, as close to the sun as Mercury is and as far from the sun as Saturn is. Would the orbits of all the other planets also be in the ecliptic?

The answer is, no. Each planet's orbit is in its own separate plane which is not quite like the plane of any other planet's orbit. Each plane crosses the ecliptic at an angle—a different angle for each one.

But then, how do we measure angles?

The ancient Babylonians worked out the system we still use. They divided any circle into 360 equal parts and we call each part a "degree."

Imagine an angle being formed by separating two lines which remain joined at one end. If you move the lines apart until one has traveled through a complete circle and rejoined the other, it will have gone through 360 degrees (or 360°). If the moving line only describes half a circle, it is 180°; only a quarter of a circle, it is 90°; and so on (see Figure 5).

As you see, anything less than ten degrees is quite a small angle. The orbital planes of the other planets cross the plane of Earth's orbit (this is called the "inclination to the ecliptic") at very small angles (see Table 8).

This shows that although the solar system isn't a perfectly flat object, it is almost flat. The planets move about in nearly the same plane.

Fig. 5—Angles

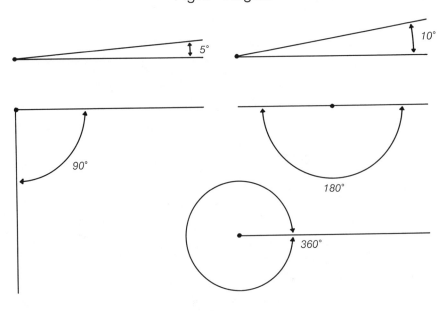

# TABLE 8

## Inclination to the Ecliptic of the Six Planets

| PLANET | INCLINATION TO THE ECLIPTIC (DEGREES) |
|---|---|
| Mercury | 7.00 |
| Venus | 3.39 |
| Earth | 0.00 |
| Mars | 1.85 |
| Jupiter | 1.30 |
| **Saturn** | **2.49** |

Imagine a planet following an orbit which is inclined to the ecliptic at a small angle. During half of its orbit it is moving above the ecliptic. Then, at some point in its orbit, it crosses the ecliptic and then moves below the ecliptic for the other half of the orbit, crossing again to move above it and so on.

The two places where the planet's orbit crosses the ecliptic are called "nodes" and they are at opposite points of the orbit. As the planet travels from one node to the other, it rises above the ecliptic more and more, till it reaches a maximum height, then drops to the other node. After that it sinks below the ecliptic more and more till it reaches a maximum depth, then rises to the other node. The maximum distance from the ecliptic, either above or below, comes halfway between the nodes.

The maximum distance above or below the ecliptic is greater as the inclination is greater. It is also greater as the distance of the planet from the sun is greater. An angle may be very small but the farther you draw out the two lines, the greater the distance by which they are separated.

We can calculate the distance from the ecliptic halfway between the nodes for each planet (see Table 9).

# TABLE 9

## Distance from the Ecliptic for the Six Planets

| PLANET | DISTANCE FROM THE ECLIPTIC | |
|--------|------------|------------|
|        | KILOMETERS | MILES      |
| Mercury | 8,520,000 | 5,290,000 |
| Venus | 6,450,000 | 4,000,000 |
| Earth | —— | —— |
| Mars | 8,050,000 | 5,000,000 |
| Jupiter | 18,500,000 | 11,500,000 |
| **Saturn** | **65,400,000** | **40,600,000** |

As you see, because of Saturn's great distance, there are places in its orbit where it moves as far from the ecliptic as Mercury is from the sun. It can get four times as far from the ecliptic as Jupiter does and eight times as far as any of the inner planets do.

This great distance up and down isn't much, though, compared to Saturn's distance from the sun. If you can imagine a model of the solar system only 50 centimeters * (20 inches) across, Saturn would only move 2.3 centimeters (0.9 inches) up and down. You could fit such a model of the original solar system very nicely into the kind of box used for pizzas—which is a good illustration of how essentially flat the solar system is.

---

* A centimeter is 1/100,000 of a kilometer, or about 2/5 of an inch.

# 2
## SATURN

**Brightness of the Sun**

In order to learn more about Saturn and its properties, we must continue to deal with all six planets and compare them. For instance, the farther a planet is from the sun, the smaller the sun appears in its sky.

The sun, as it appears to us in Earth's sky (if we look at it with the proper precautions to cut off its dangerous radiation), is a sizable ball of light. We can measure its size by calculating the angle it makes at the eye. If you imagine a straight line drawn from one side of the sun to the eye, and another straight line from the other side of the sun to the eye, those two lines will meet at an angle of about half a degree.

This means that if you imagine a number of circles, each the size of the sun, laid off against the sky side by side, it would take 720 of them to make a complete circuit of the sky. That is because there are 360 degrees in a circle and each sun-sized curve would mark off half a degree, so that there would be two such curves to each degree.

The old Babylonian custom was to divide each degree into sixty equal divisions, which we call "minutes of arc." Thus, the diameter of the sun as seen from Earth is about thirty minutes of arc, which we usually write as 30′.

Astronomers measure the angular width of the sun accurately and find it to be 31.99′ on the average. This width changes as the Earth moves along its orbit and varies its distance from the sun. When the Earth is at perihelion (on January 2) and is at its closest to the sun, the sun appears largest and then has a width of 32.50′. When the Earth is at aphelion (on July 2) and is farthest from the sun, the sun appears smallest and then has a width of 31.47′.

This change in the width of the sun in the course of the year can be measured by astronomers, but it is so small a change that people in general are not aware of it. The sun looks just about the same size every day of the year.

The sun would, of course, look considerably larger if it were viewed from Venus, which is so much closer to the sun than Earth is. It would look still larger when viewed from Mercury. It would be smaller than it seems to us if it were viewed from the outer, more distant planets (see Table 10).

# TABLE 10

## Apparent Width of the Sun
## Seen from the Six Planets

| PLANET | AVERAGE APPARENT WIDTH | |
| | MINUTES OF ARC | FROM EARTH = 1 |
| --- | --- | --- |
| Mercury | 82.6 | 2.58 |
| Venus | 44.2 | 1.38 |
| Earth | 32.0 | 1.00 |
| Mars | 21.0 | 0.66 |
| Jupiter | 6.0 | 0.19 |
| **Saturn** | **3.3** | **0.10** |

From every planet, the sun looks largest at perihelion and smallest at aphelion. If the eccentricity of a planet's orbit is very small, this change is also small. On Venus, for instance, the change in the apparent size of the sun, from perihelion to aphelion, is only half as large as the already small change we see on Earth. On Mercury, however, which has the most eccentric orbit of the six planets, there is quite a large difference. At aphelion, the apparent width of the sun is 66.6', which is about 2.1 times the width of the sun as we see it. At perihelion on Mercury, the width of the sun is an enormous 104.2', or 3.26 times as wide as we see it.

On Saturn, the change between perihelion and aphelion doesn't make much difference in the apparent size of the sun. At aphelion, the sun's apparent width shrinks to 3.0'; at perihelion it expands to 3.5'.

Actually if a circle of light in the sky is less than about 6' in diameter, it can't be clearly seen as a circle. It looks, at best, like a fat dot of light. From Jupiter, the sun can barely be made out as a tiny circle of light. From Saturn, the sun looks like a dot of light—a very brilliant and blazing star. At perihelion it looks a little brighter than at aphelion, but at all times it is starlike in appearance.

Naturally, the smaller the sun appears to be, as seen from a particular planet, the less light and heat reaches that planet in a particular time. The amount varies according to the area of the sun, which is proportional to the square of the diameter. If the sun were to increase to three times its normal width, its apparent area and the amount of radiation it would give off would be 3 × 3, or nine times its normal amount. If the sun were to shrink to ¼ its normal width, its apparent area and the amount of radiation it would give off would be ¼ × ¼, or 1/16 its normal amount. The apparent area of the sun as seen from each planet and the amount of radiation received are given in Table 11.

# TABLE 11

## Sun's Area and Radiation from the Six Planets

| PLANET | APPARENT AREA OF SUN (SQUARE MINUTES OF ARC) | RADIATION RECEIVED FROM SUN (EARTH = 1) |
|---|---|---|
| Mercury | 5,360 | 6.66 |
| Venus | 1,535 | 1.91 |
| Earth | 805 | 1.00 |
| Mars | 350 | 0.43 |
| Jupiter | 28 | 0.035 |
| **Saturn** | **8.5** | **0.011** |

The amount of radiation received is highest at perihelion and lowest at aphelion but, except for Mercury, this change doesn't amount to much. In the case of Mercury, the area of the sun is 3,480 square minutes of arc at aphelion, and the amount of radiation received then is 4.3 times what the Earth receives. At perihelion, however, the bloated sun of Mercury has an area of 8,530 square minutes of arc, at which time Mercury receives 10.6 times the radiation that the Earth receives.

As for Saturn, the amount of radiation it receives varies from 0.012 at perihelion to 0.009 at aphelion. We might as well say that wherever Saturn might be in its orbit, the amount of light and heat it receives from the sun is only about $\frac{1}{100}$ the amount that Earth gets. This means that Saturn, at least at its visible surface, is the most frigid of the six planets known to the ancients.

We mustn't view it, however, as a dim, dark planet with no light worth mentioning. Even if it only gets $\frac{1}{100}$ as much sunlight as we do, that is still quite a bit. The sun as seen from Saturn shines with a light that is 4,700 times as bright as that of the full moon as seen from Earth. The sun sends enough light to Saturn to make it gleam brightly in our telescopes, and to make it easily visible to the unaided eye.

## Brightness of the Planets

The reason we see the various planets in the sky is that each one reflects some of the sunlight that reaches it and we see that reflected sunlight.

Naturally the farther a planet is from the sun, the less light it receives; and the farther it is from us, the less of its reflected light reaches us. We would therefore expect a distant plant to appear less bright in the sky than a nearby planet does.

The brightness of objects in the sky is usually measured in "magnitudes." This system was first introduced by an ancient Greek astronomer, Hipparchus (hih-PAHR-kus, 190 B.C.–120 B.C.).

He divided the stars into six groups. The brightest were first magnitude, and those just barely visible to the unaided eye were sixth magnitude. In between were the second, third, fourth, and fifth magnitudes.

Modern astronomers measure brightness accurately and allow each magnitude to be just 2.512 times as bright as the one lower down. They can also measure magnitudes to one or even two decimal places. A star of magnitude 3.1 is 1.097 times as bright as a star of magnitude 3.2, and a star of magnitude 3.11 is 1.009 times as bright as a star of magnitude 3.12.

The brightest stars have magnitudes a little above or below 1.0. One of the dimmer first-magnitude stars can have a magnitude of 1.3; a brighter one can have a magnitude of 0.7. A few very bright stars are so bright they move up past 0.0 into the negative magnitudes. The star Sirius, which is the brightest star in the sky, has a magnitude of —1.42.

The brightness of the planets varies according to a number of factors. Naturally the farther away they are, the less bright they will be. Then, too, if only a part of the side of the planet we see is reflecting sunlight, the planet will be dimmer than it would be if its entire face were gleaming.

Since Mars, Jupiter, and Saturn are farther from the sun than Earth is, the sun is always shining on them over our shoulder so to speak, and we see them always "full" with the entire side we see gleaming with light. (Sometimes Mars looks a little lopsided since it is so close to us, we can see around it just a little to the dark side, when it is at an angle to us.)

Since Venus and Mercury are closer to the sun than we are, they sometimes show part or all of their unlit side to us, and we can see them go through all the phases that the moon does. When they are close to us, we usually see them as crescents and the closer they are, the thinner the crescent. Venus and Mercury are therefore not as bright in appearance to us as they might be.

For each planet there is some position in its orbit (relative to Earth's position in its orbit) when it shines most brightly. The brightness at such a time is given in Table 12.

As you see, the planets are as bright as the brightest stars. Saturn, at its brightest, is half as bright as Sirius; while Jupiter, at its brightest, is 2.8 times as bright as Sirius. Venus is the brightest of all the planets and shines, at its peak, with a brilliance thirteen times that of Sirius.* It is because the planets are so bright that their changing position relative to the stars was so quickly noticed by the early star-watchers.

---

* To be sure, even Venus pales in the Earth's sky in comparison to the full moon which, at its brightest, has a magnitude of —12.73 and is then 2,540 times as bright as Venus at its brightest. As for the sun, its magnitude is —26.91, and it is 470,000 times as bright as the full moon.

# TABLE 12

## Apparent Brightness of the Six Planets

| PLANET | MAXIMUM BRIGHTNESS | |
| | MAGNITUDE | SATURN = 1 |
| --- | --- | --- |
| Mercury | —0.2 | 0.6 |
| Venus | —4.22 | 24.5 |
| Earth | — | — |
| Mars | —2.02 | 3.2 |
| Jupiter | —2.55 | 5.3 |
| **Saturn** | **—0.75** | **1.0** |

(*Note: Earth is not included because it does not shine in our sky, of course, but if it could be seen from Venus it would gleam, at its brightest, with a magnitude of —5.16, and would be 2.4 times as bright as Venus appears to us and nearly 60 times as bright as Saturn appears to us.*)

Table 12 is puzzling in one way. Mars is considerably closer than Jupiter. Mars can get as close as 56,000,000 kilometers (34,800,000 miles) to Earth. This is less than a tenth of the distance of Jupiter. A ray of light going from the sun to Jupiter and back to Earth would travel a distance five times longer than one going from the sun to Mars and back to Earth. We might therefore expect that Mars would appear twenty-five times as bright as Jupiter in the sky, and by a similar calculation it would appear about eighty times as bright as Saturn in the sky. Instead Mars is only ⅗ as bright as Jupiter when both are at their brightest, and is only a little over three times as bright as Saturn. What is wrong?

The explanation is that planets come in different sizes. A large planet catches more light from the sun and reflects more than a small one would. A small planet might be surprisingly dim even though it were close to us and a large planet might be surprisingly bright even though it were far from us.

How can we tell how large a planet is? To the unaided eye, they all look like mere dots of light. If we look at them in a telescope, however, their images expand and they then look like little circles of light (or half circles or crescents in the case of Venus and Mercury). The width of these circles can be measured and if we know by how much the telescope magnifies the image, we can tell how wide the planet is to the unaided eye.

Each planet, even when it is closest to us, has a width of 1′ or less. The apparent width of each planet at its closest approach to us is given in seconds of arc in Table 13.

# TABLE 13

## Apparent Width of the Six Planets

| PLANET | MAXIMUM APPARENT WIDTH (SECONDS OF ARC) |
|---|---|
| Mercury | 12.7 |
| Venus | 64.5 |
| Earth | — |
| Mars | 25.1 |
| Jupiter | 50.0 |
| **Saturn** | **20.6** |

*(Note: Earth is not included, but as seen from Venus it would have a maximum apparent width of 71.5 seconds of arc.)*

Even though Jupiter is ten times as far away from Earth as Mars is, when both are at their closest Jupiter appears as the wider object. Even though Saturn is twenty-two times as far away from us as Mars is, when both are at their closest Saturn appears as an only slightly smaller object than Mars.

It must be that, in actual fact, Jupiter and Saturn are much larger than Mars is. In fact, knowing the apparent width of each planet and its distance, astronomers can calculate the actual diameter of each planet (see Table 14).

# TABLE 14

## Diameter of the Six Planets

| | DIAMETER | | |
| PLANET | KILOMETERS | MILES | EARTH = 1 |
| --- | --- | --- | --- |
| Mercury | 4,850 | 3,015 | 0.380 |
| Venus | 12,140 | 7,540 | 0.951 |
| Earth | 12,756 | 7,926 | 1.000 |
| Mars | 6,790 | 4,220 | 0.532 |
| Jupiter | 143,200 | 88,980 | 11.23 |
| **Saturn** | **120,000** | **74,600** | **9.41** |

As you can see, Jupiter and Saturn are giants compared to the planets of the inner solar system (see Figure 6).

Saturn's surface area is over 85 times that of Earth, and its volume is over 800 times that of Earth. If you imagined a hollow ball the size of Saturn, and if you dropped other balls the size of Earth into it and mashed them close together, you could find room inside Saturn for over eight hundred Earths.

To be sure, Jupiter is larger still, but not very much larger. It has a volume that is 1.7 times as large as Saturn's, and 1400 times that of Earth.

Now that we know how large the planets are, we can calculate how bright they are, allowing for both size and distance, and it turns out that this is not enough. We still get less light

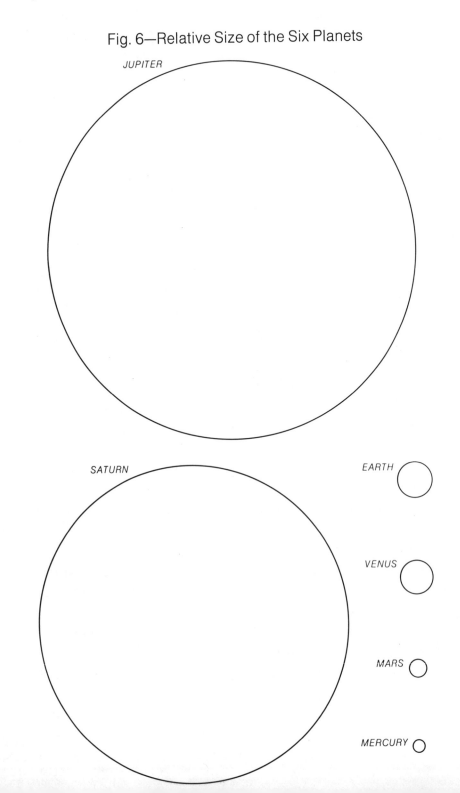

Fig. 6—Relative Size of the Six Planets

from Mars than we would expect, considering what we get from Jupiter and Saturn.

One possibility is that different planets reflect different amounts of light. If a planet's surface is made up of light-colored rocks it will reflect a larger fraction of the sunlight that falls upon it than another planet would if it had a surface made up of dark-colored rocks. If a planet's surface were covered by some icy substance or by a cloudy atmosphere, it would reflect a still larger fraction of the sunlight that falls upon it.

Knowing a planet's distance from the sun and from us, and knowing its size, astronomers can calculate how much light should reach us if the planet reflected all the light that fell on it. From the light that actually reaches us, we can tell what fraction of the light is actually reflected. This fraction is the "albedo" (al-BEE-doh) from the Latin word for "white." The albedos of the various planets are given in Table 15.

Mercury has no atmosphere and the bare rock of its surface reflects about $\frac{1}{14}$ of the light that falls on it. (This is also true of our moon.) Mars has a thin atmosphere and reflects $\frac{1}{7}$ of the light that falls on it. Earth has a thicker atmosphere, one

# TABLE 15

## Albedos of the Six Planets

| PLANET | ALBEDO |
|--------|--------|
| Mercury | 0.07 |
| Venus | 0.76 |
| Earth | 0.40 |
| Mars | 0.15 |
| Jupiter | 0.44 |
| **Saturn** | **0.42** |

which is quite cloudy, so it reflects ⅖; while Venus has an even thicker and cloudier atmosphere and reflects ¾.

From the albedo alone, we can deduce that Jupiter and Saturn must either have cloudy atmospheres or else, considering their distance from the sun, may possibly have an icy surface.


## The Spinning of the Planets

Until the invention of the telescope, the planets were seen only as dots of light. No one really knew what they were.

Once Galileo looked upon them with his telescope, however, he saw they were little orbs. Jupiter and Saturn looked like little full moons. So did Mars, although it occasionally seemed a little flattened at one side when the viewer could make out a bit of the hemisphere on which the sun was not shining. Mercury and Venus went through phases like that of the moon and would sometimes look like little half-moons or little crescents.

They were all worlds; they only looked like little dots of light because they were so far away. (When Galileo looked at the much closer moon through his telescope, it appeared so close that he could see craters, mountains, and dark places that looked like seas.)

The planets were so far away that even the use of telescopes (at least, early and primitive telescopes) showed no detail. One thing they did show, though. The outlines of Jupiter and Saturn were not circular, but elliptical. This was something quite new. The sun and the moon had shapes that were perfect circles, or something very close to that. This was also true of Mercury, Venus, and Mars. All of these were perfect spheres, or very close to that, in three dimensions. Earth itself, of course, was known to be a sphere so that if one looked at it from space it would have a circular outline.

Yet Jupiter was clearly elliptical, and Saturn even more so. In three dimensions, they would have the appearance of ellipsoids—spheres flattened at opposite sides.

The ellipsoidal shapes of Jupiter and Saturn seemed particularly interesting once Newton announced his law of universal gravitation in 1687. If a large quantity of matter gathered together, its own gravitational pull would make it come together as a sphere because, in a sphere, every piece of matter was crowded as close to the center as it could go.

If Jupiter and Saturn were ellipsoidal in shape, it meant that something was counteracting the pull of gravity in them, but not in the other planets. What could it be?

Newton himself supplied the answer. When an object rotates (spins) about some center, it tends to move in a straight line and is kept rotating only because there is some pull that continually holds it to the center. The faster the object turns, the stronger the pull must be to keep it rotating and to keep it from flying off.

This tendency to fly off is called the "centrifugal" effect, from Latin words meaning "to flee the center."

When a planet rotates, it is the gravitational pull that keeps all parts of it rotating and keeps them from flying off. The faster the planet turns, the less capable the gravitational pull is of holding all parts and there is a tendency for the planet to expand a bit as though the parts were straining at the leash.

A planet rotates about a straight line passing through its center, a line called the "axis." Different parts of the planet rotate at different speeds, depending upon how far from the axis a particular part is.

The axis crosses the surface of a planet at the north pole and the south pole, so that at the poles, the surface is not really moving, and there is no centrifugal effect there. As one goes away from the poles, the surface is making first a small circle about the axis and then, as one travels farther and farther away, the surface makes a larger and larger circle. At the equator, which is exactly halfway between the poles, a point on the surface would make the largest circle of all as the planet rotates.

The planet rotates all in one piece, however, so whether a point on the surface makes a small circle about the axis or a large circle, it takes the same time to complete that circle.

Thus, when the Earth makes one rotation, a point of 40° N. (the latitude of Philadelphia) makes a circle that is 30,700 kilometers (19,100 miles) long, while a point on the equator makes a circle that is 40,070 kilometers (24,900 miles) long. In both cases, though, the circle is completed in just twenty-four hours. That means that a point in Philadelphia is whirling about the Earth at a speed of 1,280 kilometers per hour (795 miles per hour) while a point on the equator is whirling about the earth at a speed of 1,670 kilometers per hour (1,040 miles per hour).

In general the material making up the Earth at depths beneath the equator is moving more rapidly than the material making up the Earth at depths beneath places of higher latitude. The centrifugal effect is zero at the poles and grows larger and larger for all the material between the surface and the equator as one moves away from the poles, until it is at a maximum at the equator.

For that reason, the Earth bulges away from the poles more and more until the upward bulge is greatest at the equator, and it is just this kind of bulge that would change a sphere into an ellipsoid.

A rotating planet is bound to be ellipsoidal and the longest diameter would be from any point on its equator, through its center, to the opposite point on its equator. This is the "equatorial diameter" and the planet is said to have an "equatorial bulge." The shortest diameter is from the north pole to the south pole. This is the "polar diameter" and the planet is said to be "flattened at the poles."

The first method used by astronomers to determine the period of rotation of a planet other than the Earth was to locate some marking on a planet and follow it around, timing its reappearance. This was easily done for Mars and Jupiter by the 1660s.

Saturn was a harder problem. It was so far away that it was hard to make out any spots on its surface to follow. It wasn't till 1794 that the German-English astronomer William Herschel (1738–1822) managed to make the determination.

Mercury and Venus were even harder nuts to crack and their rotation periods weren't determined till the 1960s—by studying the manner in which radio waves bounced off their surface. The rotation periods for the planets are given in Table 16.

# TABLE 16

## Rotation Periods of the Six Planets

| | PERIOD OF ROTATION | |
| --- | --- | --- |
| PLANET | HOURS | DAYS |
| Mercury | 1,409 | 58.7 |
| Venus | 5,834 | 243.1 |
| Earth | 24 | 1.00 |
| Mars | 24.62 | 1.03 |
| Jupiter | 9.83 | 0.41 |
| **Saturn** | **10.23** | **0.43** |

Despite the fact that Jupiter and Saturn are so large, it appears they turn on their axes more rapidly than the small inner planets do. We can see this if we calculate how quickly a point on the equator moves on each of these planets as in Table 17.

# TABLE 17

## Equatorial Speeds of the Six Planets

| | EQUATORIAL SPEED | |
|---|---|---|
| PLANET | KILOMETERS PER HOUR | MILES PER HOUR |
| Mercury | 10.8 | 6.7 |
| Venus | 6.5 | 4.0 |
| Earth | 1,670 | 1,040 |
| Mars | 867 | 539 |
| Jupiter | 45,765 | 28,440 |
| **Saturn** | **36,850** | **22,900** |

From the figures in Table 17, we can see why it is that Jupiter and Saturn are visibly ellipsoidal while the other planets seem to be spherical. On all planets in the table but those two, the speed of rotation is so slow that the centrifugal effect isn't large enough to counter the gravitational pull noticeably.

The diameters of the planets, as given in Table 14, are the equatorial diameters, the longest. In Table 18, polar diameters of the planets are given, the shortest ones, together with the difference in length of the two diameters.

The difference in diameters is equally distributed on either side of the planet's axis, so that Earth, for instance, has a 21.5-kilometer (13-mile) equatorial bulge on both sides; in fact, all around the mid-regions of the planet. Mars has one that is

# TABLE 18

## Polar Diameters of the Six Planets

| PLANET | POLAR DIAMETER | | DIFFERENCE IN DIAMETER | |
|---|---|---|---|---|
| | KILOMETERS | MILES | KILOMETERS | MILES |
| Mercury | 4,850 | 3,015 | 0 | 0 |
| Venus | 12,140 | 7,540 | 0 | 0 |
| Earth | 12,713 | 7,900 | 43 | 26 |
| Mars | 6,729 | 4,182 | 61 | 38 |
| Jupiter | 134,000 | 83,300 | 9,200 | 5,680 |
| **Saturn** | **107,900** | **67,100** | **13,100** | **7,500** |

slightly higher despite the fact that it spins at a slightly slower speed, because speed of rotation is not quite the only factor to be considered.

Jupiter and Saturn, and particularly the latter, have enormous equatorial bulges. Saturn's bulge everywhere in its equatorial regions is almost half the width of Earth itself, and is substantially wider than the diameter of Mercury.

Another way of demonstrating this is to measure the "oblateness" of each planet. This is calculated by taking the difference in diameters and dividing that by the length of the equatorial diameter (see Table 19). This is a measure of how far removed from the spherical a planet is.

As you see, Saturn is the most oblate of the planets listed, over thirty times as oblate as the Earth.

## *The Axial Tipping of the Planets*

When a planet is quite oblate, it is easy to see where its equator is. The equator has to lie along the major axis of the elliptical

# TABLE 19

## Oblateness of the Six Planets

| PLANET | | EARTH = 1 |
|---|---|---|
| Mercury | 0.0 | 0.0 |
| Venus | 0.0 | 0.0 |
| Earth | 0.00335 | 1.0 |
| Mars | 0.0052 | 1.55 |
| Jupiter | 0.064 | 19.1 |
| **Saturn** | **0.102** | **30.4** |

outline. You can also locate the equator by noticing the line which is parallel to the direction in which spots on the planet's surface move as the planet rotates, and is halfway between the extreme ends of the planet.

If the axis of rotation were straight up and down, at right angles to the plane of revolution around the sun, then one half of the planet stretching from the north pole to the south pole would be in sunlight and the other half in the dark. As the planet turned, every spot on the surface would experience an alternation of days and nights of equal length.

This, however, is not quite how planets actually rotate. In every case, the axis is tipped so that it does not form a right angle with the plane of the planet's revolution. It is tipped, sometimes slightly, sometimes quite a bit, from the vertical.

The axis may be tipped so that the north pole points partly toward the sun and the south pole away from the sun. If this is so, the north pole and the regions around it (how large a region depends on how far the pole is tipped) are in perpetual sunlight as the planet rotates, while the south pole and the regions around it are in perpetual night.

The regions in the neighborhood of the equator experience alternation of day and night, but the regions north of the equator have days that are longer than the nights, and the regions south of the equator have nights that are longer than the days.

It doesn't stay this way permanently, for as the planet revolves about the sun, its axis of rotation does not change its angle of tilt. Therefore, when the planet has reached the opposite point of its orbit, it is the north pole that is tipped away from the sun and the south pole that is tipped toward it. The situation is then just the reverse of what it was. The south pole has perpetual sunlight, the north pole perpetual night and so on.

When the planet is just in between the two extremes, there comes a point (two of them, on opposite sides, in the course of each revolution) where the entire globe gets a day and night of equal length (see Figure 7).

## Fig. 7—Axial Tipping and Revolution

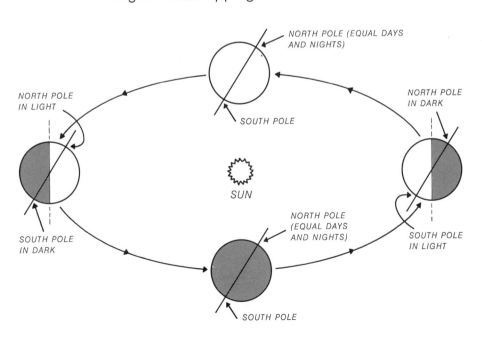

The Earth's axis is tipped 23.45° from the vertical, but the figure is different for each of the various planets (see Table 20).

## TABLE 20

## Axial Tipping of the Six Planets

| PLANET | AXIAL TIPPING (DEGREES) |
|---|---|
| Mercury | 7 |
| Venus | 3.4 |
| Earth | 23.45 |
| Mars | 23.98 |
| Jupiter | 3.08 |
| **Saturn** | **26.73** |

Of the six planets, Saturn has the greatest axial tilt. If the Earth's axis were tipped as much as Saturn's is, the noonday sun would rise higher in the summer than it does now, and sink lower in the winter, and this would be true everywhere on Earth. The difference between the seasons would be more marked.

For Saturn itself, of course, the difference is far less important than it would be for Earth. After all, the sun is so far away from Saturn and delivers so little heat in comparison to what Earth receives that it scarcely matters, as far as temperatures on Saturn are concerned, whether the sun rises a little higher or not.

# 3

---

THE
RINGS
OF
SATURN

## *The Discovery of the Rings*

When astronomers looked through the primitive telescopes of the 1600s at the planets, the appearance of Saturn troubled them. It looked quite different from anything else they could see in the sky.

The very first astronomer to notice this was Galileo himself. In 1610 he turned his small telescope on Saturn, peered at it in a puzzled way, and looked again. He did not see the simple circle of light he expected to see.

On either side of Saturn, he saw a bit of additional light. It was as though Saturn consisted of three spheres, a large one in the center and two smaller ones on either side.

Galileo had already discovered that Jupiter had four small attendant bodies that moved around it as our moon moves around the Earth. His first thought, therefore, was that there were two attendant bodies for Saturn. If that were so, though, the two small spheres should move around Saturn. Each of them should take its turn at moving behind Saturn, then in front of it, as Jupiter's attendant bodies move before and behind their planet, and as the moon (if viewed from space) would move before and behind the Earth.

This did not happen in the case of Saturn, however. Any

time Galileo looked at Saturn, he found the two small spheres on either side as though they were fixed in space. He didn't know what to make of it.

He didn't like to report what he saw because many of the astronomers of his day, who believed in older theories of the structure of the heavens, scorned Galileo's accounts of his telescopic discoveries. They insisted that what he saw through the telescope were optical illusions. The two globes on either side of Saturn struck Galileo as so bizarre that he couldn't help but wonder if they, at least, were indeed optical illusions. To report them, he thought, might give ammunition to his enemies, so he decided to keep quiet till he could work out an explanation for them.

On the other hand, he didn't want to lose the credit for being the first to see these strange structures if they really existed. What he did, then, was to send a letter to his friend, Johannes Kepler. Included in the letter was a scrambling of letters that made no sense.

If those letters were rearranged, however, they formed Latin words that, in English, would say "I have seen the outermost planet triple."

Galileo returned to Saturn now and then, and found the smaller globes getting harder and harder to see. Finally, toward the end of 1612, he couldn't see them at all and that puzzled him more than ever. "Has Saturn perhaps devoured his own children?" he growled. After all, that was what Saturn (Kronos) had done in the old Greek myths.

Later on they appeared again, but Galileo remained puzzled by them to the end of his life.

Other astronomers who looked at Saturn in those early days of the telescope also saw these odd objects on either side of the planet. The German astronomer Christoph Scheiner (SHY-ner, 1575–1650) didn't think they looked like small globes. In 1614 he described them as tiny crescents of light, with their points toward Saturn. In fact, they looked like teacup handles on each side of Saturn. (This was a better description than Galileo's, actually.)

Of course, if they were really handles fixed to Saturn, then they would turn with Saturn and would disappear when one moved behind Saturn and one moved in front of it. Even when they were visible, one on each side, they should seem to change shape as they turned. The handles, however, seemed exactly the same night after night. Could it be that Saturn did not rotate?

The first person to understand what it was that astronomers had been puzzling over for forty years was the Dutch astronomer Christian Huygens (HOY-genz, 1629–1695). He had built a better telescope than anyone before him, so that he could see Saturn more clearly and with greater magnification than anyone before him.

Using this telescope in 1656, he looked at Saturn's "handles" and decided that what he was looking at was a ring that encircled Saturn. Even if it turned around the planet, part of it would always project on either side of the planet, so that it would give the effect of motionless handles.

He wasn't completely sure that this was so, so in a report he published in 1659 he included a string of meaningless letters, as Galileo had done. When the letters were properly rearranged, they formed Latin words which, in English, were "Encircled by a ring, thin and flat, nowhere touching, inclined to the ecliptic."

Huygens had thus discovered that Saturn was encircled by a ring. It was the only planet that had such a ring about itself. In fact, nothing in the sky looked like Saturn, which, because of the ring, is usually considered the most beautiful sight one can see in a telescope.

The ring is in the plane of Saturn's equator. If Saturn's axis were straight up and down, without any tipping, then we could see the rings go straight across the center of Saturn's disc and we would see its narrow edge—like looking at a playing card held horizontal at the level of our eyes, edge on. The rings are so narrow that at the vast distance separating us from Saturn, we would then not be able to see them at all. Saturn would seem to be a simple globe, as Jupiter and Mars seem.

Saturn's axis, however, is tipped through an angle of nearly 27 degrees. That means the rings are tipped through an angle of nearly 27 degrees to the plane of Saturn's orbit about the sun. Since Saturn's orbit is nearly in the plane of Earth's orbit, that means that Saturn's rings are tipped by about that much to the plane of Earth's orbit (the ecliptic). That was one of the things that Huygens had noted in his jumbled letters.

The rings maintain their position as Saturn revolves about the sun, and that means that astronomers on Earth are fortunate enough to see the rings from different angles.

When Saturn is at one end of its orbit, we look down at the part of the ring that is in front of Saturn. The ring seems to swoop downward, leaving the globe of Saturn sticking up above. When Saturn is at the opposite end of its orbit we see the other side of the ring and look up at it. The ring then seems to swoop upward, leaving the globe of Saturn sticking down below.

Since Saturn revolves about the sun in twenty-nine and a half years, it takes nearly fifteen years for Saturn to move from one end of its orbit to the other. This means that if we see the ring sweep down in front of Saturn at a particular time, we will see it swoop up in front of the side we see fifteen years later, then down in fifteen years more and so on.

While Saturn is moving from one end of its orbit to the other, the amount of tip that *we* see in the ring changes constantly. Starting from the extreme downward swoop, it tilts slowly upward until it reaches the extreme upward swoop. Halfway in between we see it exactly edge-on. On the way back from the extreme upward swoop to the extreme downward one, it tilts slowly downward and midway between we again see it edge-on.

Twice in Saturn's swing around the sun we see the ring edge-on, which means that we see it in that fashion at intervals of a little less than fifteen years (see Figure 8).

As the ring approaches the edge-on position, it becomes harder and harder to see, and for a period of time as it passes

Fig. 8—Saturn's Rings As Seen from Earth

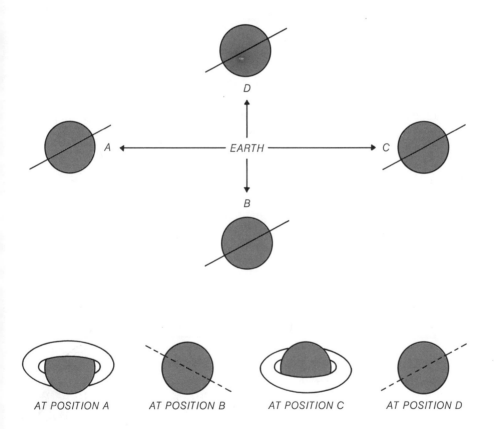

AT POSITION A    AT POSITION B    AT POSITION C    AT POSITION D

through the edge-on position, it is completely invisible. That was why Galileo, after having seen the ring in 1610 and 1611, found he could not see it in 1612.

Huygens understood this behavior of the ring, for he had seen it disappear, then reappear in 1656 as he watched. He predicted the next three times when it would disappear—in July, 1671, in March, 1685, and in December, 1700. The ring behaved exactly as predicted and that settled matters.

Other astronomers now began to observe the ring carefully. In 1675, Cassini (who, five years earlier, had measured the parallax of Mars) noticed that Saturn's ring was not just a curved sweep of light. There was a dark line all around the ring, dividing it into an outer and an inner section. The outer section was thinner and not as bright as the inner section.

It seemed that Saturn was surrounded not by a ring but by two rings, one inside the other, and ever since then people have spoken of the rings of Saturn, in the plural. The German-Russian astronomer Friedrich G. W. von Struve (SHTROO-vuh, 1793–1864) gave the rings names in 1826, but not very imaginative ones. He called the outer one Ring A and the inner one Ring B. The gap between them is "Cassini's Division."

In 1850 an American astronomer, William Cranch Bond (1789–1859), reported a dim ring still closer to Saturn than Ring B. This innermost ring is sometimes called the "crepe ring" and sometimes Ring C. There is no noticeable gap between Rings B and C.

### The Size of the Rings

If we were looking down on Saturn from out in space, a million kilometers or so above one of its poles, we would see Saturn as a partially lit circle surrounded by its rings, half of which would be in Saturn's shadow, of course. Ignoring the effects of sunlight, of day and night, Figure 9 shows how it would look.

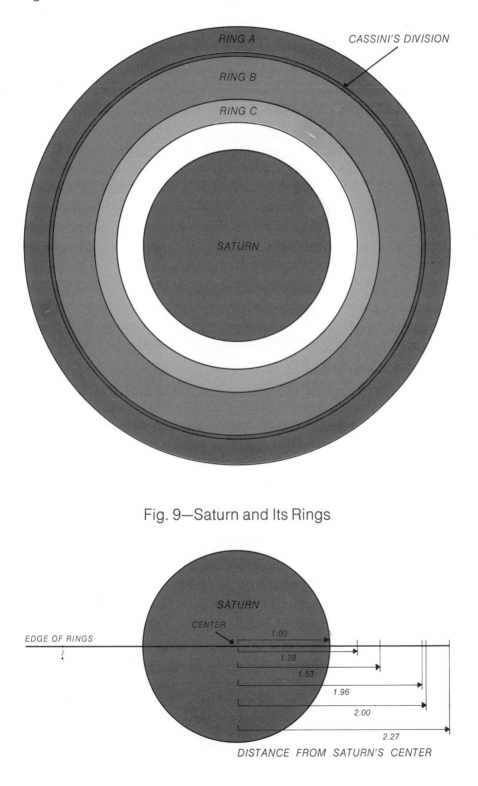

Fig. 9—Saturn and Its Rings

The distance of Saturn's surface from its center would be its equatorial radius. (A radius, as you see, has half the length of a diameter of a given circle or sphere.) The distance of the inner and outer edges of the three rings can then be given in kilometers, in miles, and in terms of the equatorial radius, as in Table 21.

# TABLE 21

## Saturn's Ring System

| | DISTANCE FROM SATURN'S CENTER | | |
| | KILOMETERS | MILES | EQUATORIAL RADII |
|---|---|---|---|
| Saturn's surface | 60,100 | 37,300 | 1.00 |
| Ring C, inner edge | 76,800 | 47,700 | 1.28 |
| Ring C, outer edge } Bing B, inner edge { | 92,000 | 57,000 | 1.53 |
| Ring B, outer edge (Cassini's Division) | 117,800 | 73,200 | 1.96 |
| Ring A, inner edge | 120,400 | 74,800 | 2.00 |
| Ring A, outer edge | 136,450 | 84,800 | 2.27 |

To picture the width of each ring, we can, as in Table 22, use Earth's diameter as a measure. As you see, the entire Earth could rest on any one of the rings without covering its entire width. In fact, two Earths side by side could rest on Ring B and not quite cover its width. It would take five Earths side by side to stretch across all three rings, counting Cassini's Division, the Division not being wide enough to allow one of the Earths to slip through.

# TABLE 22

## Width of Saturn's Rings

| | KILOMETERS | WIDTH MILES | EARTH'S DIAMETER = 1 |
|---|---|---|---|
| Ring C | 15,200 | 9,400 | 1.20 |
| Ring B | 25,800 | 15,000 | 2.03 |
| Cassini's Division | 2,600 | 1,600 | 0.20 |
| Ring A | 16,050 | 10,000 | 1.27 |
| Total | 59,650 | 36,000 | 4.70 |

Given the width of the rings, we can calculate the surface of each of the rings (above and below) and compare it with the surface of the Earth, as in Table 23.

# TABLE 23

## Area of Saturn's Rings

| | AREA (EARTH = 1) |
|---|---|
| Ring C | 31.8 |
| Ring B | 67.1 |
| Ring A | 52.3 |
| Total | 151.2 |

The ring system, in total, has a surface area 1.7 times as great as the surface of Saturn itself and 1.2 times as great as the surface of Jupiter.

The rings, however, are very thin. We still don't know exactly how thin but the most reasonable current estimate seems to be 2.5 kilometers (1.5 miles).

If we imagine the rings to be solid structures, then their total volume would be equal to that of a sphere about 5,700 kilometers (3,500 miles) in diameter, somewhat larger than that of Mercury.

## The Makeup of the Rings

Huygens, who discovered the rings, thought they were solid, because they looked solid. In fact, for over a hundred years after the discovery there were astronomers who thought they were solid objects. Some even thought that Cassini's Division was a dark marking on a luminous ring and that there was only one ring after all. (The time came, finally, when a star was seen through Cassini's Division and that was the final proof that it was a real gap.)

If the rings were solid objects, however, there would be trouble with the law of gravitation.

Imagine two bodies, such as the Earth and the moon, each exerting a gravitational pull on the other. The gravitational pull is not an unvarying one, though, because the intensity of the pull decreases with distance.

This means that the moon's pull on the side of the Earth facing it is greater than its pull on the side of the Earth away from it. This difference in pull of the moon on the Earth acts to stretch the Earth in the direction of the moon, both toward it and away from it. As a result, a mound of water from Earth's oceans builds up on the side facing the moon and on the side away from the moon.

As the Earth turns, any particular part of its shorelines moves into the mound and out of it so that water seems to creep up the shore and then down the shore twice a day. These are the tides. For that reason, the effects of a difference in gravitational pull of one body on another is called a "tidal effect."

The Earth's gravitational pull produces a tidal effect on the moon. The moon doesn't have any water, but its rocky substance is stretched in the direction of the Earth. As the moon turns, this tidal effect slows its rotation until the moon makes just one turn about its axis every time it revolves about the Earth. Once that happens the stretched mounds of rock are always directly facing the Earth and directly away from it and that is a stable situation. The moon's rotation has been fixed by tidal action.

The Earth's rotation is also slowing as a result of the moon's tidal effect. The moon is a much smaller body, so its gravitational field is much weaker than Earth's is. Then, too, the Earth as the larger body is much harder to slow down. It will therefore be many billions of years before the Earth's rotation slows to the point where one side always faces the moon as it turns and the Earth's day, too, becomes just one month long. (When that time comes the month will be longer, for the moon will be farther away and it will take longer for it to revolve around the Earth.)

A smaller body is less affected by tidal effects than a larger body is. Thus, although the Earth is 81 times as massive as the moon, the tidal effect the moon experiences is not 81 times that which the Earth experiences. The tidal effect on the moon is larger, but not 81 times larger. Since the moon is smaller than the Earth, there is less difference of gravitational pull with distance across its body than across Earth's.

Then, too, the closer two bodies are, the stronger the tidal effects. The tidal effect increases as the inverse cube of the distance. If the distance between the moon and the Earth were ½ what it is, the tidal effect would be $2 \times 2 \times 2$, or 8 times as great. If the distance were ⅓ what it is, the tidal effect would be $3 \times 3 \times 3$, or 27 times as great. Similarly, if the distance between the moon and the Earth were 3 times what it is, the tidal effect would be $\frac{1}{3} \times \frac{1}{3} \times \frac{1}{3}$, or $\frac{1}{27}$ times as great.

In other words, as two bodies approach each other the tidal effect mounts very rapidly.

The first person to think about tidal effects with respect to the rings of Saturn was the French astronomer Pierre Simon de Laplace (lah-PLAHS, 1749–1827).

In 1785 Laplace pointed out that objects move more slowly about a planet the farther away from the planet they are. For instance, the innermost part of the rings, under Saturn's strong gravitational pull, would turn in only $\frac{2}{5}$ of the time the outermost part would—since the outermost part would be under the weaker pull of a considerably more distant Saturn.

If the ring were solid, it would have to turn in one piece and every part of it would have to complete its turn in the same period of time. We could suppose that the whole thing would turn at some average speed. Driven by gravity, though, the inner parts would strain forward to take up their natural faster speed, and the outer parts would strain backward to take up their natural slower speed. The tidal effect thus set up would break up the ring, even if it were made of the strongest known substance.

Laplace suggested that what surrounded Saturn was actually a set of numerous very narrow rings, one set inside another. Each one would be so narrow that the tidal effects across it would be too small to worry about. Cassini's Division would, by his view, be only one of very many divisions. It would just happen to be the widest, so that it was the first to be seen.

For seventy years after that, astronomers tried to find other dividing lines in the rings, but at the vast distance of Saturn these would be hard to see, even if they were there. Sometimes there were reports of some having been sighted, but there was no general agreement on such sightings.

In 1855 a Scottish mathematician, James Clerk Maxwell (1831–1879), showed that Laplace's analysis wasn't complete enough. Even narrow rings wouldn't do. The only way that Saturn's rings could withstand tidal effects would be for them to be made up of vast numbers of small bodies, each one too small for tidal effects to be important.

In Maxwell's view, Saturn's rings are actually a cloud of small bodies, each perhaps no more than a few centimeters across, and all circling Saturn.

There are so many fragments in the cloud that from a distance as great as Saturn's they seem to melt together and look like a solid ring, just as the separate grains of sand seem to melt together and form a solid stretch of beach if viewed from a distance.

Maxwell's reasoning was unanswerable and his view is accepted to this day. The discovery of Ring C was a strong point in its favor. If Maxwell was right, then Ring C was very dim because it had fewer fragments in it than had Rings A and B. This was so, for stars would sometimes be seen through Ring C.

## The Origin of the Rings

In 1850 a French astronomer, Edouard Roche (RUSH, 1820–1883), tried to work out what would happen if the moon could somehow be imagined to circle nearer and nearer the Earth.

If it did so, then, the tidal effects of the moon and the Earth on each other would become stronger and stronger. As the Earth is the larger body, it would produce a greater effect on the moon than the moon would produce on the Earth. Furthermore the Earth, with its more intense gravitation, would be able to withstand a given strain better than the moon could. Therefore, in any such approach it would be the moon that would suffer more.

Eventually, if the moon came close enough its structure

would not withstand the pull of the tidal effect and it would begin to break up. It would continue to break into smaller and smaller pieces until the pieces were too small to be bothered much by tidal effects—at least as far as breakup was involved.

Tidal effect could then alter the orbit of the moon fragments. The pieces of the moon might, to begin with, circle the Earth in various planes, according to whatever force was exerted by the particular breakup that produced them. Little by little, though, tidal effects would force them to circle the Earth in the plane of Earth's equator. The fragments would stretch out into a wide, thin structure just like Saturn's rings.

That seemed a possible explanation for Saturn's rings. Perhaps an attendant body, like our moon, had for one reason or another gotten too close to Saturn and had been pulled apart by tidal effects. Or perhaps when a planet first formed there was matter all around it that collected together to form such subsidiary bodies, but if there were such matter too close to a planet, tidal effects would keep it from collecting into a large body and it would stay in fragments.

Roche calculated that, provided certain simplifying assumptions were made, sizable bodies would break up if they approached more closely to the planet they circled than 2.44 times the radius of that planet. Or, if fragments already existed closer to the planet than that, they would not be able to coalesce.

For that reason, 2.44 times the equatorial radius of any planet is called the "Roche limit" for that planet (see Table 24). As it happens, Saturn's rings are at a distance of 1.28 times the equatorial radius of Saturn at their innermost edge and 2.27 times the radius at the outermost edge. The entire ring system is inside the Roche limit.

Since Saturn's rings are composed of small particles, they may be mostly empty space, even though they look solid from a distance. The particles of the rings fill about one third of the

# TABLE 24

## Radius and Roche Limit of the Six Planets

| PLANET | EQUATORIAL RADIUS | | ROCHE LIMIT | |
|---|---|---|---|---|
| | KILOMETERS | MILES | KILOMETERS | MILES |
| Mercury | 2,425 | 1,507 | 5,917 | 3,677 |
| Venus | 6,070 | 3,770 | 14,810 | 9,200 |
| Earth | 6,378 | 3,963 | 15,562 | 9,670 |
| Mars | 3,395 | 2,110 | 8,284 | 5,150 |
| Jupiter | 71,600 | 44,490 | 174,700 | 108,600 |
| **Saturn** | **60,000** | **37,300** | **146,400** | **91,000** |

volume of the rings, the remaining two thirds being empty space.

If all the material in the rings were collected into a sphere, then, the size of that sphere would be less than the one we calculated on the assumption that the rings were solid. The actual diameter of the sphere would be only about 4,000 kilometers (2,500 miles), or about the size of our moon.

# 4

## TITAN

### *Mass and Density*

Until the telescope came into use, exactly eight members of
the solar system were known, each of them observed since the
dawn of recorded history and, in many cases, for uncounted
centuries earlier. These included the sun itself, the six planets
that circled it, and, finally, the moon that circled the Earth.

The moon is smaller than any of the planets, but not very
much smaller. Whereas Mercury, for instance, has a diameter
of 4,850 kilometers (3,010 miles), the moon has a diameter of
3,476 kilometers (2,160 miles).

Could planets other than Earth also have attendant bodies
circling them? They might, but if the attendants were small,
they would be much less bright than the planets themselves.
They might be too dim to be seen; or, if they were bright enough
to be seen by themselves, they might be so close to the planet
that they would be drowned in the glare of the larger and
brighter body.

There was therefore no hope of seeing such bodies until the
telescope was invented (and, for that matter, it never occurred
to astronomers that such unseen bodies might exist).

Once the telescope was turned on the sky, the discovery of
attendant bodies followed almost at once. In January 1610

Galileo looked at Jupiter with his small telescope and found four attendants. These were named Io (EYE-oh), Europa (yoo-ROH-puh), Ganymede (GAN-ih-meed), and Callisto (ca-LIS-toh) in order outward from Jupiter. These names were those of three nymphs with whom Jupiter (Zeus) had fallen in love and a prince (Ganymede), who was his cupbearer in the Greek myths.

They were each bright enough to be seen as dim stars even without a telescope, if Jupiter's light could be blocked out. In the presence of Jupiter, however, the telescope was required.

When Kepler heard of the discovery, he termed the attendants "satellites" from a Latin word meaning "attendant." The objects Galileo discovered were therefore four satellites of Jupiter (sometimes lumped together as the "Galilean satellites" in his honor). Using this term, we can speak of the moon as the satellite of Earth.

The discovery of Jupiter's satellites raised the known members of the solar system from 8 to 12, a jump of 50 percent. What's more, these satellites were the very first members of the solar system whose discovery could be placed in a particular year and ascribed to a particular person.

For nearly half a century the Galilean satellites were the only satellites known, except for our moon.

But then, in 1655 Huygens (who, at the same time, was working out the real meaning of the "globes" or "cup handles" on either side of Saturn) discovered a small gleam of light near Saturn. He followed it from night to night and found that it was moving around Saturn.

In 1656 Huygens announced that Saturn, like Jupiter and Earth, possessed a satellite.

Huygens did not give the satellite a name but simply called it "Saturn's moon." Two centuries later, however, in 1858, the English astronomer John Herschel (1792–1871) gave it one.

In the Greek myths the gods of the generation led by Kronos

(Saturn), who preceded Zeus (Jupiter), were called the **Titans**. Herschel therefore called the satellite Titan. It wasn't really a good name because it didn't represent a mythical individual, but rather a whole group of individuals. However, the name stuck.

The discovery of Titan was important, since once a planet is known to have a satellite its mass (or the quantity of matter it contains) can be determined.

To begin with, Titan goes around Saturn once every 15.95 days.

Then, once Saturn's distance was worked out, the distance of Titan from its planet could also be determined from the apparent distance as seen in the telescope. It turned out that Titan's distance from the center of Saturn was 1,222,000 kilometers (759,000 miles).

Our moon goes around the Earth in 27.32 days but its distance from the Earth's center is only 384,390 kilometers (238,-860 miles). From the law of gravitation we can calculate that if the moon were as far from the Earth as Titan is from Saturn, the moon would go around the Earth once in 154.5 days.

The moon, in other words, would take roughly ten times as long to go around the Earth as it takes Titan to go around Saturn, if both were at equal distances from their planet. By gravitational theory, if Saturn drives its satellite ten times as fast as Earth drives its, then Saturn's gravitational field (and therefore its mass) is roughly 10 × 10, or 100 times stronger than Earth's.

The mass of the other planets in terms of Earth's mass can be worked out, too, when they have satellites. Those planets that don't have satellites must have their masses worked out in other, less convenient ways, and the results are given in Table 25.

As you see, Saturn is the second most massive of the six planets, but not a very good second. It is only one third as

# TABLE 25

## Masses of the Six Planets

| PLANET | MASS (EARTH = 1) |
|--------|------------------|
| Mercury | 0.0558 |
| Venus | 0.8150 |
| Earth | 1.0000 |
| Mars | 0.1074 |
| Jupiter | 317.9 |
| **Saturn** | **95.1** |

massive as Jupiter. Jupiter, all by itself, has 76.6 percent of the mass of the six planets and Saturn has 22.9 percent. The remaining four planets, including Earth, have only 0.5 percent of the mass.

Yet, even though Jupiter and Saturn are so massive they are, in a way, surprisingly low in mass. Saturn, for instance, has a volume over 800 times that of the Earth. You might think it should therefore contain over 800 times as much matter as Earth—but it does not. It contains less than 100 times as much matter as Earth.

This means that matter is less closely packed together in Saturn than in Earth. This packing is called "density." The more matter there is in a volume of a particular size, the denser that matter is.

We can measure mass in kilograms (or in pounds, where 1 kilogram is equal to 2.2 pounds), and we can measure volume in cubic meters (or cubic feet, where 1 cubic meter is equal to 35.3 cubic feet). We can say that a certain piece of matter has a density of so many kilograms per cubic meter (or so many pounds per cubic foot).

Water, for instance, has a density of 1,000 kilograms per cubic meter (62.43 pounds per cubic foot).

Different rocks in the Earth's crust have different densities, but the average density of the Earth's crust is considerably greater than that of water. It comes to about 2800 kilograms per cubic meter (175 pounds per cubic foot).

The interior of the Earth is considerably denser than the crust and it is calculated that the average density of the Earth's globe as a whole is 5,518 kilograms per cubic meter (344.5 pounds per cubic foot). The average density of each of the six planets is given in Table 26.

# TABLE 26

## Densities of the Six Planets

| | DENSITY | | | |
| PLANET | KILOGRAMS PER CUBIC METER | POUNDS PER CUBIC FOOT | EARTH = 1 | WATER = 1 |
| --- | --- | --- | --- | --- |
| Mercury | 5,600 | 349.6 | 1.015 | 5.6 |
| Venus | 5,200 | 324.6 | 0.943 | 5.2 |
| Earth | 5,518 | 344.5 | 1.000 | 5.5 |
| Mars | 3,950 | 246.6 | 0.716 | 4.0 |
| Jupiter | 1,314 | 82.0 | 0.238 | 1.3 |
| **Saturn** | **704** | **44.0** | **0.128** | **0.7** |

Scientists are quite sure that the core of the Earth is a huge ball of molten iron (together with some quantity of the similar metal, nickel). Around it is a large "mantle" made of rock that is denser than the rocks on the surface. This structure suggested for Earth fits, among other things, the average density figure.

Venus and Mercury are almost surely built up of the same metal and rock structure and all three are of similar average density.

Mars is only seven tenths as dense as the three planets closer to the sun than it is, and that seems to be because it lacks much in the way of a metal core and is, for the most part, a ball of rock. (The same seems to be true of the moon.)

Jupiter is, on the average, only a quarter as dense as the Earth is. That means only a small portion of its structure can be either metal or rock. It must consist largely of still less dense material. The same must be true of Saturn, and to an even greater extent, since Saturn is only one half as dense as Jupiter, and only one eighth as dense as Earth.

In fact, Saturn is the only one of the six planets—indeed, the only known sizable body of any classification in the solar system—that is less dense than water. If there were a vast ocean of water, and if planets held together when placed in such an ocean, only Saturn would float. The rest would sink.

## The Structure of Planets

In order to understand the meaning of Saturn's phenomenally low density, as first revealed through the distance and motion of Titan, let's consider how the solar system got its start. The current belief is that it began as a huge swirling mass of dust and gas, which gradually drew together and condensed under the pull of its own gravity.

Most of it collected into a dense central ball that was so massive that the atoms at its center were smashed by the pressures induced by its gravitational pull inward. The atomic nuclei at the center of the atoms, no longer shielded by the outer atomic layers, began to collide and combine with each other, giving off energy in the process. The whole central ball began to glow and to radiate light and heat. In short, it became the sun.

While this was happening, the dust and gas on the outskirts of the forming sun collected into planetary bodies at various distances from the sun, the planets being quite small compared to the central sun. (Even Jupiter has only $\frac{1}{1000}$ the mass of the sun.)

The cloud out of which the solar system was formed would naturally have been made up of the same kind of substances that make up the universe generally. Astronomers have ways of determining the chemical structure of the sun and of other stars, as well as of the dust and gas between the stars. They have therefore come to some conclusions as to that makeup. In Table 27 are listed the chemical elements of the universe

## TABLE 27

### Abundance of the Elements

| ELEMENT | NUMBER OF ATOMS (SILICON = 10,000) |
|---|---|
| Hydrogen | 400,000,000 |
| Helium | 31,000,000 |
| Oxygen | 215,000 |
| Neon | 86,000 |
| Nitrogen | 66,000 |
| Carbon | 35,000 |
| Silicon | 10,000 |
| Magnesium | 9,100 |
| Iron | 6,000 |
| Sulfur | 3,750 |
| Argon | 1,500 |
| Aluminum | 950 |
| (all other elements) | (about 1,400) |

(each made up of a distinctive type of atom) in order of decreasing quantity.

As you see, the universe is essentially hydrogen and helium, the two elements with the simplest atoms. Together, hydrogen and helium make up 99.9 percent of all the atoms of the universe. Only one atom out of a thousand is anything else.

Both hydrogen and helium are gases and, along with neon and argon, do not become liquids until very low temperatures are reached. Even at great distances from the sun, hydrogen and helium remain gases. We can therefore place these elements together under the classification of "gases."

The atoms of helium, neon, and argon do not combine either with each other or with the atoms of other elements. Hydrogen atoms will, however, combine with themselves in pairs to form hydrogen molecules or to form other molecules with the atoms of other elements.

Oxygen, nitrogen, carbon, and sulfur are made up of atoms which are all likely to combine with hydrogen atoms when hydrogen atoms are present in overwhelming quantity. Each oxygen atom combines with two hydrogen atoms to form a molecule of water. Each nitrogen atom combines with three hydrogen atoms to form a molecule of ammonia. Each carbon atom combines with four hydrogen atoms to form a molecule of methane. Each sulfur atom combines with two hydrogen atoms to form hydrogen sulfide.

These substances—water, ammonia, methane, and hydrogen sulfide—are gases at warm temperatures, but become liquids and even solids at temperatures that are cold, but not cold enough to make hydrogen or helium liquid or solid.

Of these substances, the one that freezes under the mildest conditions is water. Even on Earth, temperatures can grow cold enough to freeze water into ice. The other substances won't freeze until lower temperatures are reached, but once frozen, they resemble ice in appearance. All these substances can be referred to as ices. (If we mean the substance we ordinarily refer to as ice, we can call it water ice.)

Silicon combines with oxygen much more easily than with hydrogen. Magnesium and aluminum combine readily with the silicon-oxygen combination, and these four elements together are the chief basis of the rocky materials (silicates) we are familiar with.

Finally, iron is the most common of the metals, and in planets such as the Earth we have large metallic cores that are chiefly iron.

We can group the common elements in this way and in Table 28 list them by classes.

# TABLE 28

## Substances Making up the Solar System

| SUBSTANCE | ATOM NUMBER (SILICON = 10,000) | RELATIVE MASS (TOTAL = 110) |
|---|---|---|
| Gases | 431,000,000 | 98.6 |
| Ices | 300,000 | 1.0 |
| Rocks | 40,000 | 0.3 |
| Metals | 7,000 | 0.1 |

The atoms of metals and rocks hang together by chemical forces that are stronger than gravity—at least in small bodies no more massive than the Earth. They do so at all temperatures up to white heat.

Gases, on the other hand, cling to planetary bodies only through gravitational force and are therefore much less securely part of a planet. If ices are warmed, they vaporize to gases and they too cling to a planet only by gravitational force.

What's more, the warmer the surface of a planet, the more rapidly the atoms and atom combinations of gases move, and the more readily they escape from the planet into outer space despite the gravitational pull.

When planets form close to the sun, rock and metal hang together without any trouble. A planet made up of rock and metal can form even if close enough to the sun to be at a perpetual red-hot temperature. In that case, though, it can't be very large since the mass of rock and metal is only, at best, $\frac{1}{250}$ of the mass of the original cloud out of which the solar system formed.

Such small bodies don't develop enough of a gravitational field to hold on to the gases and the vaporized ices, especially since these are warmed and made elusive by the nearness of the sun. Mercury has none to speak of; Mars has a little; Earth and Venus have a little more.

Far from the sun, though, the ices are solid and frigid and their atoms and molecules hold together by chemical forces as well. With the ices, planets can grow two or three times as massive as planets built out of rock and metal alone. That would give them enough gravitational pull to collect the matter around them with greater efficiency and to grow still greater at the expense of the smaller, warmer planets which then do not grow even as large as they might were it not for the larger, colder planets' efficiency in growing.

The large planets could even collect the very rich supply of gases and hold them gravitationally . . . which would make them still larger with still more intense gravitational fields . . . which would make them capable of holding the gases even more efficiently . . . which would make them still larger. . . .

In this way, the distant planets grew to be enormous giants, but ended up mostly gases and ices, which are lower in density than rock and metal are. In fact, Jupiter and Saturn are mostly hydrogen which has the lowest density of all. For this reason,

Jupiter and Saturn are sometimes called "gas giants" and that is why their density is so much lower than that of the rock-and-metal worlds of the inner solar system.

The density of the gas giants would be lower still were it not that they developed into such large and massive planets that their gravitational pull squeezed and compressed the gases of which they were composed far more tightly than they ever could be on Earth and made them far more dense. Still, even under the pull of their large gravities, Jupiter and Saturn remained considerably less dense than Earth.

It is quite certain, then, that what seem to us to be the surfaces of Jupiter and Saturn are not at all the kind of solid surface we think of in connection with the inner planets. What we see as a surface is but the top of a cloud layer and under it a dense, thick atmosphere must stretch downward.* It is these clouds that give Jupiter and Saturn their high albedos (see Table 15 on page 49).

It is not possible to learn the details of what lies beneath the cloud layer merely by looking at the gas giants with a telescope.

A better way is to study the light they radiate. Light consists of tiny waves of different lengths. These waves can be sorted out by an instrument called a spectroscope. Since Jupiter and Saturn reflect the light from the sun, all the wavelengths present in sunlight should also be present in the light from Jupiter and Saturn. If any wavelengths are missing it is because they were absorbed by materials in the planets' atmospheres. Every chemical substance absorbs some special wavelengths and no others, so the missing wavelengths act as "fingerprints" to indicate the presence of those substances.

In 1932 the German astronomer Rupert Wildt (VILT, 1905–

---

* For convenience, we will sometimes refer to the "surface" of Jupiter or Saturn as though it were solid like the surface of Earth, rather than the top of a cloud layer.

1976) detected the presence of ammonia and methane in the atmospheres of Jupiter and Saturn in this way. Undoubtedly other ices were present also, in gaseous, liquid, or solid form (or, more likely, in all three). Unfortunately, hydrogen and helium don't absorb visible light strongly so they could not be detected, but astronomers were quite certain for other reasons that those gases were present.

On December 3, 1973, a rocket probe, Pioneer 10, passed only 135,000 kilometers (85,000 miles) from Jupiter's surface, and on December 2, 1974, Pioneer 11 passed at a distance of 42,000 kilometers (26,000 miles) from its surface.

From the data they sent back, it now seems quite certain that Jupiter is a ball of hydrogen with some helium added. The visible cloud surface of Jupiter is quite frigid, its temperature far below the freezing point of water, but as one moves beneath it, the temperature climbs to great heights. In the uppermost layers of Jupiter, where the temperatures are mild and even cold, there are water, ammonia, methane, hydrogen sulfide and some more complicated compounds of carbon, oxygen, sulfur, nitrogen and hydrogen in smaller quantities.

These probes are now moving on toward Saturn, and in not too long a time we may be getting some information concerning that planet. Meanwhile, however, it seems reasonable to suppose that Saturn is like Jupiter in structure.

Saturn, too, is mostly hydrogen plus a little helium. It, too, must have ices in its upper layers. Both planets may have rock-and-metal cores at the very center, but, if so, Saturn's must be much smaller and less tightly compressed than Jupiter's, which would be why Saturn is only half as dense as Jupiter.

## Surface Gravity

Since Saturn has a gravitational field that is 95 times as intense as the Earth's, we might expect that Saturn would pull an object placed at a certain distance 95 times as forcefully as Earth would pull that same object at that same distance.

An object resting on Saturn's "surface," however, is not at the same distance from the planet's center that it would be if it were resting on Earth's surface. Saturn's surface is much farther from its center than Earth's surface is from its center.

For that reason, Saturn's "surface gravity" is not 95 times as great as Earth's. In fact, the weakening effect of the greater distance reduces Saturn's surface gravity to not much higher than Earth's (see Table 29).

# TABLE 29

## Surface Gravity of the Six Planets

| PLANET | SURFACE GRAVITY (EARTH = 1) |
|---|---|
| Mercury | 0.38 |
| Venus | 0.90 |
| Earth | 1.00 |
| Mars | 0.38 |
| Jupiter | 2.68 |
| **Saturn** | **1.15** |

Despite this, Saturn's greater mass cannot be entirely discounted even at its surface.

The pull of gravity decreases as the square of the distance. In other words, if you double your distance from the Earth, Earth's pull is only ½ × ½, or ¼ its original strength. If you increase your distance to three times what it was, Earth's pull is only ⅓ × ⅓, or ⅑ what it was.

When you are on the surface of the Earth, you are 6,370

kilometers (3,900 miles) from the center. If you moved 6,370 kilometers above the surface, you would be twice as far from the center as you had been and gravitational pull would be only ¼ as strong as it was. If you moved 12,740 kilometers above Earth's surface, you would be three times as far from the center as you had been and the gravitational pull would be only ⅑ as strong as it was.

When you are on the surface of Saturn, you are 60,000 kilometers (37,300 miles) from its center. If you move 6,370 kilometers above the surface, you have not doubled the distance from Saturn's center, you have increased it only by 10 percent. Saturn's gravitational pull is still ⅚ of what it was at the surface.

In other words, Saturn's surface gravity may not be much more than that of Earth, but Saturn's gravitational pull decreases far less rapidly than Earth's does as one moves away from the planet.

If something is thrown upward from the surface of a planet, it moves upward at a certain speed to begin with. This speed decreases steadily as a result of the planet's gravitational pull. Finally, the upward speed decreases to zero, and then becomes a downward speed. The object falls more and more rapidly till it hits the planet's surface once again.

The faster an object is thrown upward, the longer it will take for that upward speed to diminish to zero, and the greater will be the height reached by the object before it begins to fall.

If the planet's gravitational pull were constant all the way up, then no matter how rapidly you forced an object upward to begin with, its speed would still eventually dwindle to zero, and it would sooner or later come down.

The planet's gravitational pull, however, decreases with distance from the planet. If you could throw an object fast enough, the steadily decreasing pull of the planet's gravitation, as the object rose higher and higher, would never quite wear away all its speed. The object would then keep moving away from the planet forever and would escape. The minimum velocity at which this is possible is the "escape velocity" and this plays an important role in rocketry.

If you were sending a rocket up from Saturn's cloud surface at a velocity great enough to allow it to escape from Earth, that would not be enough to allow it to escape from Saturn. Saturn's gravitational pull decreases with increasing distance much more slowly than Earth's. Therefore the rocket must go with greater speed and must reach greater heights for it to get the benefit of the much slower weakening of Saturn's pull. Saturn's escape velocity would therefore have to be considerably higher than that of Earth (see Table 30).

# TABLE 30

## Escape Velocity from the Six Planets

| | ESCAPE VELOCITY | | |
| PLANET | KILOMETERS PER SECOND | MILES PER SECOND | EARTH = 1 |
| --- | --- | --- | --- |
| Mercury | 4.3 | 2.7 | 0.38 |
| Venus | 10.3 | 6.4 | 0.92 |
| Earth | 11.2 | 7.0 | 1.00 |
| Mars | 5.0 | 3.1 | 0.45 |
| Jupiter | 59.5 | 37.0 | 5.31 |
| **Saturn** | **35.6** | **22.1** | **3.18** |

### The Size of the Satellites

When Huygens discovered Titan, it was the dimmest member of the solar system that had yet been discovered. It was considerably dimmer than the Galilean satellites (see Table 31), but not extraordinarily dim considering its great distance.

# TABLE 31

## Apparent Brightness of the Six Satellites

| SATELLITE | MAGNITUDE (MAXIMUM) | APPARENT BRIGHTNESS (TITAN = 1) |
|---|---|---|
| Moon | −12.6 | 230,000,000. |
| Ganymede | 4.9 | 22.9 |
| Io | 5.3 | 15.9 |
| Europa | 5.7 | 11.0 |
| Callisto | 6.1 | 7.6 |
| Titan | 8.3 | 1.0 |

While planets seemed to come in radically different sizes (compare Jupiter and Mercury), the first satellites discovered seemed to be rather similar in size and it was no surprise that Titan turned out to be not too different in size from the other known satellites. It would have been more surprising if it were different.

The actual size of Titan was not easy to work out, however. The size of the Galilean satellites of Jupiter had not been easy to determine, considering their great distance and the difficulty of measuring their width when that distance made them appear so tiny even in the best telescopes. And Titan was twice as far as the Galileans, and therefore in a given telescope appeared to have only half the diameter.

Eventually estimates were made as to the diameter, but they were subject to correction. On March 29, 1974, for instance, the moon moved in front of Saturn. As it did so, it cut off the light of Titan, too. Modern instruments could determine accurately when the light began to fade—when the moon touched the near side of Titan. The instruments could also tell when the light finally sank to zero—when the moon touched the far side of Titan and covered it completely. The speed at which the moon moved was known, so the exact apparent size of Titan could be determined. Knowing that and its distance, its exact actual size could be worked out and it was found to be some 800 kilometers (500 miles) greater than had been thought.

In Table 32 are listed the diameters of the six satellites.

# TABLE 32

## Diameters of the Six Satellites

| | DIAMETER | | |
| SATELLITE | KILOMETERS | MILES | MOON = 1 |
|---|---|---|---|
| Titan | 5,800 | 3,600 | 1.67 |
| Ganymede | 5,220 | 3,240 | 1.50 |
| Callisto | 4,890 | 3,040 | 1.41 |
| Io | 3,636 | 2,260 | 1.05 |
| Moon | 3,476 | 2,160 | 1.00 |
| Europa | 3,060 | 1,900 | 0.88 |

The results of the 1974 observation made it clear that Titan was the largest of the six satellites, which made its name curiously, and rather unexpectedly, appropriate. The word "Titan" is not only the name of the band of gods led by Kronos (Saturn), but it has also come to mean anything gigantic because the Titans were supposed to be of gigantic size. The largest satellite is therefore appropriately named Titan.

We can see this all the better if we consider the volumes of the satellites rather than their diameters. The volume of a sphere varies as the cube of the diameter. If one sphere has two times the diameter of a second, the first has $2 \times 2 \times 2$, or eight times the volume of the second. The volumes give us a more accurate picture of differences in size than mere diameters do (see Table 33).

# TABLE 33

## Volumes of the Six Satellites

| | VOLUME | |
| SATELLITE | (MOON = 1) | (MERCURY = 1) |
| --- | --- | --- |
| Titan | 4.65 | 1.67 |
| Ganymede | 3.39 | 1.22 |
| Callisto | 2.78 | 1.00 |
| Io | 1.14 | 0.41 |
| Moon | 1.00 | 0.36 |
| Europa | 0.68 | 0.24 |

As you can see from Table 33, the volume of Titan is 1⅜ that of Ganymede, the next in line.

An odd point is that Mercury, the smallest of the planets, has a diameter of 4,890 kilometers (3,040 miles) and is just as wide, and as voluminous, as the satellite Callisto. That means, however, that two satellites, Titan and Ganymede, are larger than the smallest planet. Titan has a diameter 1.19 times that of Mercury, and a volume 1.67 times as great.

Another point to remember is that of the six satellites, four belong to the single planet Jupiter. Titan may be larger than any one of the Galilean satellites, but if we add the volumes of the four Galilean satellites, we find that Jupiter's total satellite volume is 1.7 times that of Titan, and eight times that of the moon.

But then it is only fair to point out that Jupiter is the largest planet and that when it formed, there must have been more material generally out of which to form satellites on the outskirts. Perhaps we ought to consider how large a satellite is relative to the planet it circles (see Table 34).

## TABLE 34

### Volumes of the Six Satellites
### Relative to Their Planets

| SATELLITE | VOLUME (MILLIONTHS OF THE VOLUME OF THE PLANET IT CIRCLES) |
|---|---|
| Moon | 20,435 |
| Titan | 131.1 |
| Ganymede | 53.6 |
| Callisto | 44.0 |
| Io | 18.0 |
| Europa | 10.6 |

We can see at once that in terms of the size of its primary, Titan is much more voluminous than any of the Galilean satellites and, indeed, just a bit larger than all four Galileans put together. And yet Titan cannot boast pride of place in this, for it is (perhaps unexpectedly) dwarfed by the moon. Compared to the planet it circles, the moon is far and away the largest of the six satellites.

In fact, one might ask how a planet as small as Earth could manage to form a satellite almost as large as any produced during the formation of such giants as Jupiter and Saturn. There is, as yet, no answer to this, and it is only one of the reasons that the origin of the moon is such an interesting, and puzzling, problem to astronomers.

Of course, volume can be misleading in some ways. A small amount of matter can be spread over a large volume and vice versa. In some ways, it is mass that is more fundamental.

It isn't easy to measure the mass of a satellite, however. One can determine the mass of a planet from the distance and movement of the satellites that circle it. In principle, one can do the same in reverse, since the planet moves in response to the satellite's gravitational field. A planet, however, is generally so much more massive than a satellite that the planetary motions of this sort, which are correspondingly smaller, are impossible to detect and measure.

For that reason the mass of a satellite must be judged by other methods: by the effect, for instance, of the pull of one satellite on another. The result is that in most cases, determinations of mass have been uncertain for any satellite but our moon. In recent years, however, things have been improving in this respect. The passage of Pioneer 10 and Pioneer 11 past Jupiter have given us better figures for the mass of the Galilean satellites, for instance (see Table 35).

Where mass is concerned, Titan must yield pride of place. Ganymede, slightly smaller than Titan in diameter, is nevertheless more massive. Notice that both Ganymede and Titan are each roughly twice as massive as our moon.

From the standpoint of mass, however, Mercury need no longer suffer humiliation. There may be three satellites that rival or surpass it in volume but not one of those three is as massive. Mercury is 2.2 times as massive as Ganymede and 2.4 times as massive as Titan.

The reason for this, of course, is that Mercury is a rock-and-metal world, which makes it unusually dense. In fact, there are only three large rock-and-metal worlds in the solar system and they are Mercury, Venus, and Earth. None of the satellites, as

# TABLE 35

## Masses of the Six Satellites

|  | MASS | |
| SATELLITE | MOON = 1 | MERCURY = 1 |
| --- | --- | --- |
| Ganymede | 2.027 | 0.47 |
| Titan | 1.905 | 0.42 |
| Callisto | 1.448 | 0.32 |
| Io | 1.213 | 0.27 |
| Moon | 1.000 | 0.22 |
| Europa | 0.663 | 0.15 |

far as we know, have metallic cores and for that reason their densities are considerably lower than those of the three dense planets (see Table 36).

# TABLE 36

## Densities of the Six Satellites

|  | DENSITY | |
| SATELLITE | EARTH = 1 | MOON = 1 |
| --- | --- | --- |
| Io | 0.642 | 1.06 |
| Moon | 0.605 | 1.00 |
| Europa | 0.585 | 0.97 |
| Ganymede | 0.362 | 0.60 |
| Callisto | 0.315 | 0.52 |
| Titan | 0.253 | 0.42 |

The Galilean satellites decrease in denseness as one moves outward from Jupiter. Io is a little denser than the moon, Europa a little less dense than the moon. Ganymede is three fifths as dense as the moon, and Callisto only half as dense.

It may be that when Jupiter first formed it was quite hot, so that at the distance of the nearer Galileans the ices were in gaseous form and could not be collected by the rocky material that was forming Io and Europa. Ganymede and Callisto were far enough from Jupiter for their temperature to be low enough to collect the ices. Because the ices make up more of the original cloud that formed the bodies of the solar system, Ganymede and Callisto are larger than the inner Galileans.

Titan's distance from Saturn is somewhat greater than Ganymede's from Jupiter, and Saturn must have been less warm than Jupiter. Titan must have been cold enough to pick up an unusual quantity of the ices and to have grown larger and less dense than any of the Galileans.

Knowing the mass and volume of the satellites, we can calculate the surface gravity for each of them (see Table 37) and the escape velocity (see Table 38).

Titan's low density accounts for its having the lowest surface gravity of any of the six satellites. Its surface gravity is such that a person weighing 72 kilograms (158 pounds) on Earth would weigh only 12 kilograms (26.4 pounds) on the moon, and only 8 kilograms (17.6 pounds) on Titan.

Since diameter plays a part in the calculation of escape velocities, Titan escapes being at the bottom of the list in that respect and comes out just ahead of Europa, the smallest of the Galileans.

The size of the six satellites can be looked at in yet another way. How large would each look if it were seen from the surface of the planet it circles (if, again, we consider the top of the cloud layer of Jupiter or Saturn a surface in the Earthly sense)? This is given in Table 39.

# TABLE 37

## Surface Gravity of the Six Satellites

| | SURFACE GRAVITY | |
|---|---|---|
| SATELLITE | EARTH = 1 | MOON = 1 |
| Io | 0.184 | 1.11 |
| Moon | 0.166 | 1.00 |
| Europa | 0.149 | 0.90 |
| Ganymede | 0.146 | 0.88 |
| Callisto | 0.117 | 0.70 |
| Titan | 0.111 | 0.67 |

# TABLE 38

## Escape Velocity from the Six Satellites

| | ESCAPE VELOCITY | | |
|---|---|---|---|
| SATELLITE | KILOMETERS PER SECOND | MILES PER SECOND | EARTH = 1 |
| Ganymede | 2.75 | 1.71 | 0.25 |
| Io | 2.56 | 1.60 | 0.23 |
| Callisto | 2.38 | 1.48 | 0.21 |
| Moon | 2.38 | 1.48 | 0.21 |
| Titan | 2.25 | 1.40 | 0.20 |
| Europa | 2.09 | 1.30 | 0.19 |

# TABLE 39

## Size of the Six Satellites as Seen from Their Planets

| SATELLITE | APPARENT DIAMETER (MINUTES OF ARC) | APPARENT AREA (MOON = 1) |
|---|---|---|
| Moon | 31.1 | 1.00 |
| Io | 29.4 | 0.90 |
| Ganymede | 17.0 | 0.30 |
| Titan | 16.5 | 0.28 |
| Europa | 15.9 | 0.25 |
| Callisto | 8.6 | 0.076 |

None of the other satellites looms as large in the sky of its planet as our moon does, although Io is close. What's more, none is nearly as bright as the moon; since the other satellites are much farther from the sun than the moon is, they receive far less light to reflect.

It may be, for instance, that Titan has an albedo equal to that of Callisto and, therefore, twice as large as that of the moon. Despite this doubled ability to reflect light compared to the moon, if we take into account its greater distance from the sun and its smaller appearance in Saturn's sky, it turns out that Titan would shine in Saturn's sky with only 1/160 the brightness of the full moon in ours. The magnitude of Titan at its brightest, as seen in Saturn's sky, would be —7.1, or about 14.2 times as bright as Venus appears in our sky.

## Titan's Atmosphere

Various bodies in the solar system have atmospheres—that is, layers of gas clinging to their surface. Jupiter and Saturn have huge atmospheres, of course, since they consist almost entirely of gaseous materials, or materials that would be gaseous if not compressed by their powerful gravitational fields.

Earth has an atmosphere, too, as we know: one that consists of 78 percent nitrogen, 21 percent oxygen, and 1 percent argon. There is enough of these gases, and they are sufficiently compressed by Earth's gravitational field, to produce a pressure of 10,333 kilograms per square meter of surface (14.7 pounds per square inch).

Venus has an atmosphere, too: one that is mostly carbon dioxide and that is about ninety times as dense as Earth's.

Bodies with a gravitational field smaller than those of Earth and Venus, or that are warmer, or both, have less chance of retaining gases and therefore have thinner atmospheres.

Mars, for instance, with a surface gravity only ⅖ that of Earth's has but a thin atmosphere, one with pressure only 0.006 times that of Earth's and, like that of Venus, mostly carbon dioxide in composition.

Mercury has the same surface gravity as Mars has, but is much warmer than Mars. Since hot gases are far more difficult to hold than cold gases are, Mercury has no significant atmosphere at all.

Neither does the moon, which is cooler than Mercury, but also smaller.

Rocky or metallic objects considerably smaller than the moon would have no atmospheres at any temperature. A small, cold body made up of ices might have those ices vaporize to gas if the body were somehow warmed up. It would then gain an atmosphere but it would not be able to hold on to it. No body considerably smaller than the moon could hold on to an atmosphere permanently, even if one should form.

But what about objects as big as the moon or somewhat larger, which are farther from the sun and therefore colder? What about the large satellites of Jupiter and Saturn?

The Galilean satellites of Jupiter have no significant atmospheres, but Titan is another story.

In 1944 the Dutch-American astronomer Gerard Peter Kuiper (KOY-per, 1905–1973) was able to detect an undeniable atmosphere about Titan and found it to consist of methane. What's more, the atmosphere seems to be a substantial one, very likely denser than that of Mars.

Titan is the only satellite so far known to have an atmosphere; it is the smallest body in the solar system so far known to have an atmosphere; it is the only body in the solar system so far known to have an atmosphere that is largely methane. That makes Titan unique on three counts.

There is no clear evidence, as yet, of anything other than methane in Titan's atmosphere, but it is likely that a little hydrogen is present and some substances more complicated than methane as well.

The methane molecule is made up of one atom of carbon and four atoms of hydrogen, which is usually written with the chemical formula $CH_4$. Carbon atoms can combine with each other easily, so that molecules can form with two or more carbon atoms to which various numbers of hydrogen atoms are attached. There is some indication that the gases ethane ($C_2H_6$) and ethylene ($C_2H_4$) may be present in small quantities in Titan's atmosphere.

Still more complicated hydrocarbons (molecules made up of carbon and hydrogen atoms) may be responsible for the fact that Titan appears orange in color. An orange cloud of hydrocarbons may completely hide its solid surface.

Hydrocarbons with several carbon atoms liquefy more easily than methane does and we can imagine that Titan might have a hydrocarbon ocean on its surface. We might as well call it a gasoline ocean, for gasoline is made up of liquid hydrocarbons.

There is no real evidence of this so far, but it is an interesting speculation. Perhaps the probes now on their way to Saturn may give us some new information which will help us to understand Titan a little better and allow us to make sense of this completely one-of-a-kind world.

Indeed, a probe may someday actually be sent out to land on Titan. With Titan's combination of low gravity and an atmosphere it is the easiest world in the whole solar system to land upon. And if its complicated hydrocarbons have combined with other atoms such as nitrogen, oxygen, sulfur, and phosphorus, it may be that forms of life might exist on it. This is not very likely, of course, but it would be interesting to check on the matter.

# 5

## THE SATELLITES OF SATURN

### *The Discovery of Saturn's Satellites*

When Huygens discovered Titan in 1655, he couldn't help but notice there were now six planets known (Mercury, Venus, Earth, Mars, Jupiter, and Saturn) and six satellites (Moon, Io, Europa, Ganymede, Callisto, and Titan).

This seemed a very neat arrangement to him, and so it might have seemed to anyone steeped in biblical lore. The sun, with twelve smaller bodies circling it, might have seemed like Jacob and his twelve sons or Jesus and his twelve apostles. In any case, Huygens gave it as his opinion, in 1659, that no more heavenly bodies would be discovered in the solar system.

Scientists should not, however, attach too much importance to neat arrangements of numbers without other evidence to support their theories. Although Huygens himself never found any additional bodies, Cassini (the astronomer who had discovered the gap in Saturn's rings) located no fewer than four more satellites of Saturn while Huygens was still alive. Cassini did not give them names but eventually John Herschel, who named Titan, also named Cassini's satellites.

On October 25, 1671, Cassini discovered the first of his four satellites. It was farther from Saturn than Titan was, and it was named for Iapetus (eye-AP-ih-tus) who, in the Greek myths, was a brother of Kronos (Saturn) and therefore one of the Titans. Iapetus was described as the father of Prometheus, who according to one legend first formed human beings.

On December 23, 1672, Cassini found another satellite, one that was closer to Saturn than Titan was, and it was named Rhea (REE-uh). She was a Titaness, the sister and wife of Kronos (Saturn) and the mother of Zeus (Jupiter).

Then on March 21, 1684, Cassini discovered two more satellites that were still closer to Saturn than Rhea was. Of these the outer one was Dione (digh-OH-nee), a Titaness who, in the Greek myths, was the mother of Aphrodite (Venus). The inner one was Tethys (TEE-this), another of the Titanesses, and an ancient goddess of the sea.

As a result of Cassini's discoveries, Saturn was known to have five satellites, while Jupiter's known satellites still stood at the four discovered by Galileo three quarters of a century before. Saturn's margin of superiority stretched out farther when in August and September of 1789, William Herschel (the father of John Herschel) discovered two more satellites, closer to Saturn than any of the others, raising the total to seven.

These new satellites were not named after Titans or Titanesses but after another variety of enemies of Zeus. After the defeat of Kronos (Saturn) and his Titans, the Greek myths tell of a new generation of gigantic beings who came into existence and warred against Zeus (Jupiter). They, too, were defeated. Among the leaders of these giants were Mimas (MIGH-mas) and Enceladus (en-SEL-uh-dus), and these names were given to the two new satellites.

Then, on October 16, 1848, W. C. Bond (the discoverer of Ring C) detected still another satellite of Saturn, this one between Titan and Iapetus. It was named Hyperion, after still another of the Titans—the father of Helios, the sun-god.

That meant there were no fewer than eight satellites known to be circling Saturn; twice as many as the number circling Jupiter, which still remained at four.

In 1877, when two tiny satellites were discovered to be circling Mars, there was once again an interesting situation as far as numbers were concerned.

Mercury and Venus had no satellites; Earth had one; Mars had two; Jupiter had four; Saturn had eight. It was very neat. Starting with Earth and working outward, each planet had twice as many satellites as the one before.

This neat arrangement was spoiled on September 9, 1892, when the American astronomer Edward Emerson Barnard (1857–1923) discovered a fifth satellite of Jupiter, closer to that planet than any of the Galileans, and considerably smaller than any of the Galileans (which was why it took so long to discover it, especially when it was so close to the overpowering brightness of Jupiter).

On August 16, 1898, however, the American astronomer William Henry Pickering (1858–1938) discovered a ninth satellite of Saturn, one that was farther out than any of the previous eight. He named it Phoebe, another of the Titaness sisters of Kronos (Saturn).

Phoebe was the first satellite to be discovered by photography, and Jupiter's fifth was the last to have been discovered with the unaided eye.

The score of satellites was now nine for Saturn against five for Jupiter.

The use of better and better telescopes and of better and better photographic techniques made it possible to detect very small satellites circling Jupiter at distances much greater than those of the Galilean satellites. By 1914, four of these small outer satellites of Jupiter had been discovered and the score stood nine satellites apiece for Jupiter and Saturn.

Nothing new was discovered for Saturn in the way of such small satellites. Even if they existed, Saturn is twice as far away from us as Jupiter is, and it was therefore much harder to detect small bodies circling Saturn than similar bodies circling Jupiter.

In 1938 two more small satellites were discovered to be circling Jupiter, and in 1951 still another was, and these put Jupiter in the lead, 12 to 9.

Then in December 1967 a French astronomer, Audouin Dollfus (dol-FOOS), located a tenth satellite of Saturn. It was nearer to Saturn than even Mimas was, and circled Saturn just beyond the outside edge of the rings. In fact, the reason it had never been seen through the nearly two centuries since Mimas had been discovered was that the brightness of the rings had drowned it out. It was only every fifteen years, when the rings were seen edge-on and disappeared, that this tenth satellite had a chance to be caught. December 1967 was one of those periods of ring disappearance and Dollfus managed to spot the satellite.

Dollfus named this new satellite after Janus who, in the myths, was neither a Titan nor a Titaness. In fact, he was not a Greek god at all; he was a Roman god with no Greek counterpart. Janus was the Roman god of gates and doorways, which is why we call people who guard the entrances of houses "janitors." Because of the association of Janus with doors and gates, he is considered the god of entrances and exits, of beginnings and ending, so that the first month of the year, which begins the year and is the entrance to it, is called "January."

Dollfus reasoned that the new satellite was the first of the ten in the order of distance from Saturn and the last of the ten in order of discovery, so why not name it after the god of beginnings and endings.

Since 1967, no new Saturnian satellites have been discovered by astronomers, but at least one, possibly two, have been discovered for Jupiter. The score stands: Jupiter thirteen (or fourteen), Saturn ten.

In Table 40, the ten satellites of Saturn are listed in order

# TABLE 40

## Satellites of Saturn

| SATELLITE | YEAR OF DISCOVERY | DISCOVERER |
|-----------|-------------------|------------|
| Janus | 1967 | Dollfuss |
| Mimas | 1789 | Herschel |
| Enceladus | 1789 | Herschel |
| Tethys | 1684 | Cassini |
| Dione | 1684 | Cassini |
| Rhea | 1672 | Cassini |
| Titan | 1655 | Huygens |
| Hyperion | 1848 | Bond |
| Iapetus | 1671 | Cassini |
| Phoebe | 1898 | Pickering |

of distance from Saturn, with the year of discovery and the name of the discoverer given for each.

## The Orbits of Saturn's Satellites

Since the distance of Saturn from ourselves is known, the actual distance of each satellite from Saturn is easily calculated from the apparent distance of the satellite from the planet and is given in Table 41. The rings are included in the table.

For successive satellites from the rings to Rhea, there is a steadily increasing distance with no great leaps. There is, how-

# TABLE 41

## Distance of Saturn's Satellites

| | AVERAGE DISTANCE FROM SATURN'S CENTER | | |
|---|---|---|---|
| SATELLITE | KILOMETERS | MILES | SATURN'S RADIUS =1 |
| Ring (inner edge) | 76,800 | 47,700 | 1.28 |
| Ring (outer edge) | 136,450 | 84,800 | 2.00 |
| Janus | 159,000 | 99,000 | 2.65 |
| Mimas | 186,000 | 116,000 | 3.09 |
| Enceladus | 238,000 | 148,000 | 3.96 |
| Tethys | 295,000 | 183,000 | 4.91 |
| Dione | 377,000 | 234,000 | 6.27 |
| Rhea | 527,000 | 327,000 | 8.77 |
| Titan | 1,222,000 | 759,000 | 20.33 |
| Hyperion | 1,483,000 | 928,000 | 24.68 |
| Iapetus | 3,550,000 | 2,206,000 | 59.06 |
| Phoebe | 12,950,000 | 8,050,000 | 215.5 |

ever, an unusual gap between Rhea and Titan, another between Hyperion and Iapetus, and still another between Iapetus and Phoebe. This makes it very difficult to show Saturn's satellite system to scale in a single diagram. If you make the diagram small enough to include the outermost satellites, it is difficult to make the innermost satellites with clear orbits. Therefore the system must be shown in three separate diagrams (Figures 10, 11, and 12).

While Phoebe circles Saturn at an enormous distance, thirty-four times the distance of the moon from the Earth, this is not a record for the solar system.

One of the satellites of Jupiter, the ninth to be discovered and

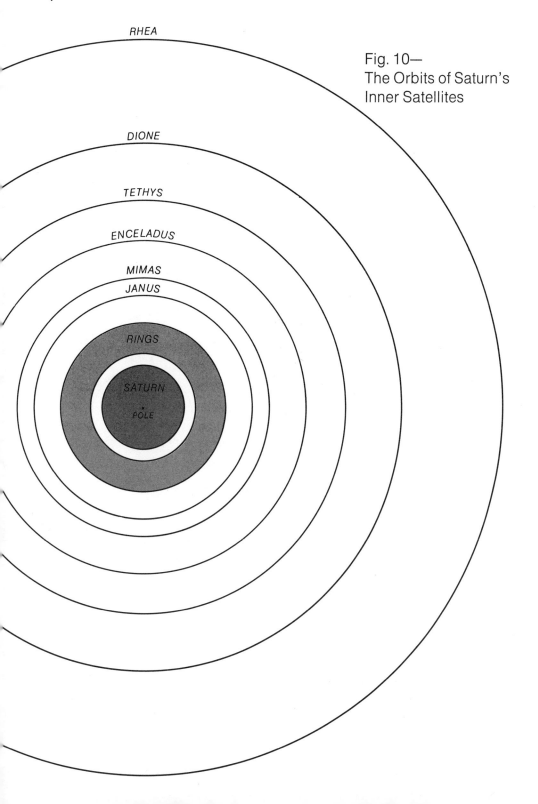

Fig. 10—
The Orbits of Saturn's
Inner Satellites

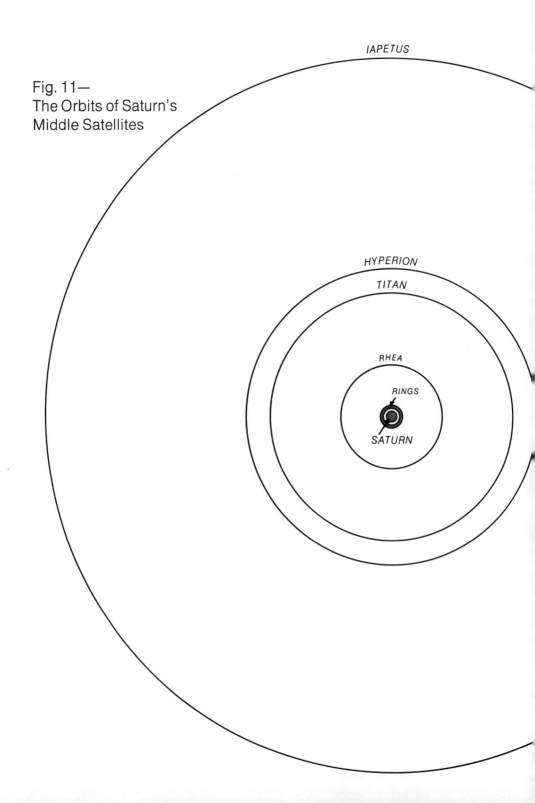

Fig. 11—
The Orbits of Saturn's
Middle Satellites

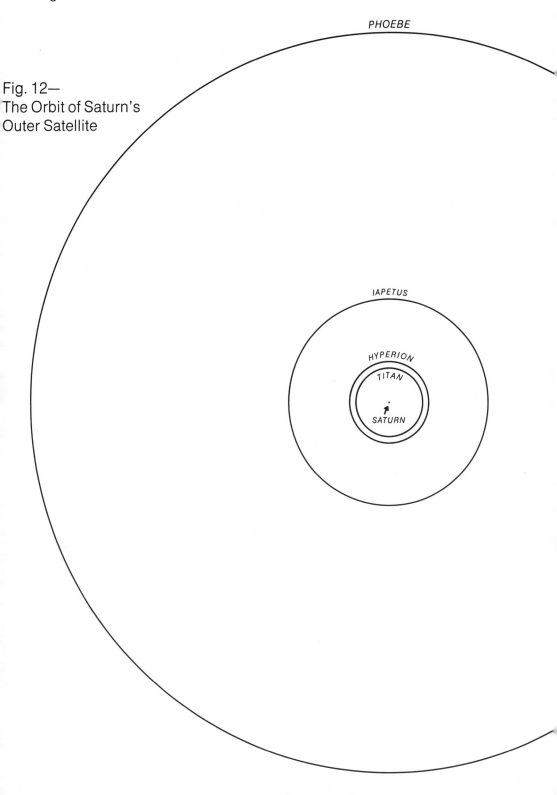

Fig. 12—
The Orbit of Saturn's
Outer Satellite

therefore usually known as J-IX, has the farthest average distance from the planet it circles—23,600,000 kilometers (14,-700,000 miles). J-IX is 1.8 times as far from Jupiter as Phoebe is from Saturn.

Naturally, the farther a satellite is from the planet it circles, the longer its period of revolution (see Table 42).

## TABLE 42

### Period of Revolution of Saturn's Satellites

| SATELLITE | PERIOD OF REVOLUTION | | ORBITAL SPEED | |
|---|---|---|---|---|
| | HOURS | DAYS | KILOMETERS PER SECOND | MILES PER SECOND |
| Rings (inner edge) | 6.05 | 0.252 | 22.2 | 13.3 |
| Rings (outer edge) | 14.26 | 0.594 | 16.7 | 10.4 |
| Janus | 17.98 | 0.749 | 15.5 | 9.6 |
| Mimas | 22.61 | 0.942 | 14.4 | 8.9 |
| Enceladus | 32.88 | 1.370 | 12.6 | 7.9 |
| Tethys | 45.31 | 1.888 | 11.3 | 7.1 |
| Dione | 65.69 | 2.737 | 10.0 | 6.2 |
| Rhea | 106.0 | 4.418 | 8.7 | 5.4 |
| Titan | | 15.945 | 5.6 | 3.5 |
| Hyperion | | 21.277 | 5.1 | 3.1 |
| Iapetus | | 79.331 | 3.3 | 2.0 |
| Phoebe | | 550.33 | 1.7 | 1.1 |

If we consider the innermost of Saturn's satellites, Janus, we see that it circles Saturn in just about 18 hours. This is an extraordinarily short period of revolution. Mercury, the closest planet to the sun, takes 88 days to complete its revolution, and the moon takes 27.3 days to complete its revolution about the Earth.

Janus, nevertheless, does not hold the record. Jupiter's nearest satellite, Amalthea (uh-MAL-thee-uh), the one discovered by Barnard, completes its revolution in 10 hours; while Phobos (FOH-bos), which is Mars's inner satellite, completes its in 7⅔ hours.

However, the particles in Saturn's rings each individually circle Saturn, and the closer they are to Saturn, the faster they move, the shorter their orbit, and the more quickly they complete one revolution. At the innermost edge of the rings, the particles circle Saturn in just about 6 hours. This is the fastest known natural period of revolution in the solar system.

The eight innermost satellites of Saturn have a shorter period of revolution than our moon does. Iapetus, however, takes nearly three times as long to circle Saturn as the moon takes to circle the Earth. Phoebe takes twenty times as long, making one revolution about Saturn in 1.5 years.

That is not a record, either. Jupiter's four outermost satellites all take longer than that to circle Jupiter. The record for Jupiter's satellites (and for all satellites so far known) is again J-IX, which circles Jupiter once every 2.08 years.

The orbital speed of the satellites is an indication of Saturn's large gravitational field. Even distant Phoebe is whipped about Saturn at a greater speed than the Earth is capable of driving the moon. The moon's orbital speed is, on the average, only 1.02 kilometers per second (0.64 miles per second).

When a planet forms, and the material on the outskirts comes together to form satellites, the tendency is for the satellites to form in the plane of the planet's equator, and to go about the planet very nearly in circles.

If a satellite starts off a little askew for any reason, with its orbit not quite in the planet's equator or with its orbit not quite circular, tidal forces tend to bring it into line. The closer a satellite is to the primary, the more effectively do the tidal forces tend to make its orbit equatorial and circular.

Saturn's rings, for instance, are exactly in the plane of Saturn's equator and are exactly circular. As for the orbits of the satellites themselves, the extent to which they are elliptical rather than circular is demonstrated by their eccentricity (see Table 43).

# TABLE 43

## Orbital Eccentricity of Saturn's Satellites

| SATELLITE | ECCENTRICITY |
|---|---|
| Janus | 0.00 |
| Mimas | 0.02 |
| Enceladus | 0.004 |
| Tethys | 0.000 |
| Dione | 0.002 |
| Rhea | 0.001 |
| Titan | 0.029 |
| Hyperion | 0.104 |
| Iapetus | 0.028 |
| Phoebe | 0.163 |

The innermost satellites have orbits that are almost perfectly circular. Only Hyperion and Phoebe have orbits that are more elliptical than that of the moon, and Phoebe's is the most elliptical, which is not surprising since it is the outermost.

Because of the eccentricity of Phoebe's orbit, it comes as close as 10,830,000 kilometers (6,370,000 miles) to Saturn at one end of its orbit and as far as 15,060,000 kilometers (9,360,000 miles) at the opposite end (see Figure 13).

Even at its farthest point from Saturn, Phoebe does not set records. It does not, at its farthest, attain the average distance from Jupiter of any of that giant planet's outermost satellites.

Fig. 13—Saturn and Phoebe

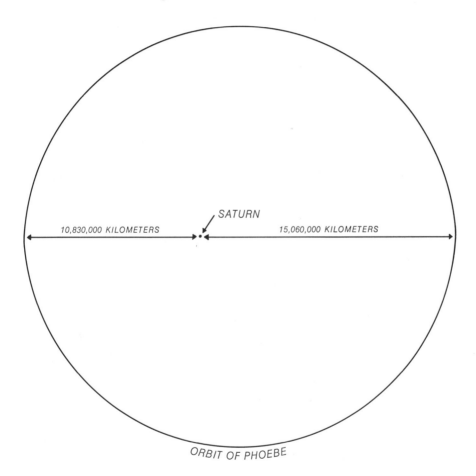

SATURN

10,830,000 KILOMETERS    15,060,000 KILOMETERS

ORBIT OF PHOEBE

Consider, for instance, J-VIII, which has an average distance from Jupiter of just a trifle less than that of J-IX, but which has a large eccentricity of 0.40. This means that J-VIII swoops in toward Jupiter at one end of its orbit, approaching as closely as 14,100,000 kilometers (8,800,000 miles). At the opposite end of its orbit, however, J-VIII moves to a distance of 32,900,000 kilometers (20,400,000 miles), more than twice as far as Phoebe ever gets from Saturn. No other satellite in the solar system ever moves as far from its planet as J-VIII does.

When J-VIII is at its farthest from Jupiter it is moving in its orbit at a speed of only 1.91 kilometers per second (1.19 miles per second). Phoebe, at *its* farthest, is moving more slowly, thanks to Saturn's smaller gravitational field, at only 1.27 kilometers per second (0.79 miles per second). Neither, however, moves as slowly as our own moon does, even when each is at its farthest point and moving most slowly.

But what about the orbital inclination? If we're going to consider that, we'll have to think about the direction in which a satellite revolves about its primary.

Imagine yourself far above the north pole of a planet, such as the Earth. If we look down upon the Earth from this position, Earth rotates in a counterclockwise direction. The moon moves around the Earth in the same direction. Both the Earth's rotation and the moon's revolution about the Earth are examples of "direct motion."

If a planet, when viewed from a position high above Earth's north pole, rotated about its axis in a clockwise direction, or if a satellite revolved about the planet in a clockwise direction, then those would be examples of "retrograde motion" (from Latin words meaning "backward steps").

Almost all motions in the solar system are direct motion and that makes sense. When the solar system was forming, the original cloud of dust and gas must have been turning in this way so that all the parts are still turning that way.

Now imagine a satellite to be revolving about its planet in direct motion, but with its plane of revolution inclined to the plane of the planet's equator more and more while the satellite continues to move in the same direction. Eventually, when it is tipped through 90 degrees, it is moving in a plane at right angles to the equatorial plane. When it is tipped further, through an angle of 180 degrees, the plane of revolution is back in the equatorial plane, but now the satellite is moving in the retrograde direction (see Figure 14).

What this means is that a satellite in any orbital plane that is tipped less than 90 degrees to the equatorial plane of its planet can be said to be in direct motion. If the orbital plane is tipped between 90 and 180 degrees to the equatorial plane it can be said to be in retrograde motion.

Now let us consider the orbital inclination of Saturn's satellites (see Table 44). As you see, the rings and the seven

Fig. 14—Orbital Inclinations

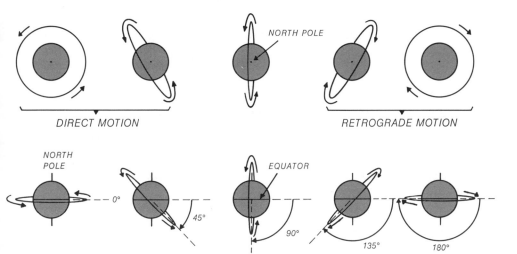

DIRECT MOTION

NORTH POLE

RETROGRADE MOTION

NORTH POLE

0°

45°

EQUATOR

90°

135°

180°

# TABLE 44

## Orbital Inclination of Saturn's Satellites

| SATELLITE | ORBITAL INCLINATION (DEGREES) |
|---|---|
| Rings | 0.00 |
| Janus | 0.00 |
| Mimas | 1.52 |
| Enceladus | 0.02 |
| Tethys | 1.09 |
| Dione | 0.02 |
| Rhea | 0.35 |
| Titan | 0.33 |
| Hyperion | 0.50 |
| Iapetus | 15. |
| Phoebe | 150. |

innermost satellites are scarcely tipped at all to Saturn's equatorial plane and to the plane of the rings. This is not true of the two outermost satellites. Iapetus has the plane of its orbit tipped 15 degrees to the equatorial plane of Saturn, while Phoebe's orbital inclination is a whopping 150 degrees (see Figure 15). Phoebe's motion about Saturn is retrograde, the only one of the satellites for which that is true.

Phoebe is not, however, unique in this respect. The four outermost of Jupiter's satellites all have retrograde motions in their revolution about Jupiter. The orbital inclination of two of them is even greater than Phoebe's: that of J-IX is 156 degrees and of J-XI, 163 degrees.

Why should Phoebe and Jupiter's outermost satellites be revolving in a retrograde manner? Were they not part of the original clouds of dust and gas that coalesced to form the

Fig. 15—Phoebe the Retrograde Satellite

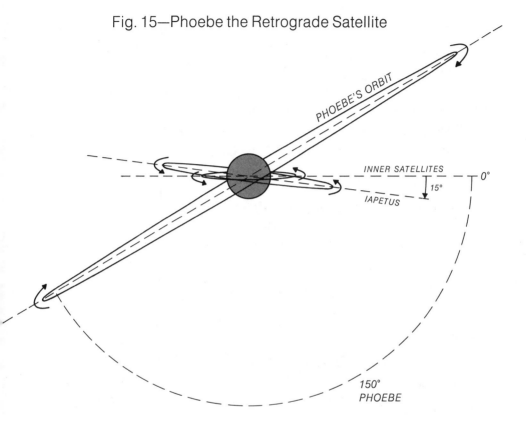

planets and their satellites? And if that cloud was revolving in direct fashion so that the planet and all the inner satellites are moving directly, why should these outermost satellites be going the wrong way on a one-way street?

Astronomers suspect that Phoebe was *not* part of the original cloud of dust and gas that coalesced to form Saturn and its other satellites. Phoebe was, perhaps a small body that had an independent orbit of its own about the sun. Its orbit occasionally brought it a little too close to Saturn a long time after that planet and its satellites had formed. It may have approached under conditions that allowed it to be trapped in Saturn's gravitational field and to move into a new orbit that took it around Saturn.

It turns out that when astronomers calculate the probability of such capture (not very great, actually) the chance of its happening is greater if the object can move into a retrograde orbit. Very likely, then, Phoebe, and all of Jupiter's small, distant satellites, are captured objects.

### The Skies of Saturn's Satellites

From all of Saturn's satellites, Saturn itself must be a magnificent sight. In Table 45 the size of Saturn is given as seen from each of its satellites.

# TABLE 45

## Size of Saturn as Seen from Its Satellites

| SATELLITE | WIDTH (DEGREES) | AREA (OUR MOON = 1) | BRIGHTNESS (OUR MOON = 1) |
|---|---|---|---|
| Janus | 41.4 | 6,390 | 492 |
| Mimas | 35.8 | 4,780 | 368 |
| Enceladus | 28.3 | 2,990 | 230 |
| Tethys | 23.0 | 1,970 | 152 |
| Dione | 18.1 | 1,220 | 94 |
| Rhea | 13.0 | 630 | 48.5 |
| Titan | 5.64 | 118 | 9.1 |
| Hyperion | 4.63 | 80 | 6.2 |
| Iapetus | 1.93 | 13.9 | 1.1 |
| Phoebe | 0.52 | 1.00 | 0.08 |

Giant Saturn is, from every satellite, the largest object in the sky, far larger than the sun. From distant Phoebe, the farthest of the satellites, Saturn, to the unaided eye, appears precisely the size of the moon as seen from Earth. From the inner satellites, Saturn is, of course, seen as larger than our moon. From Janus, it stretches a horrendous 41.4 degrees across the sky. If the lower end of Saturn, as seen from Janus, touched the horizon, the upper end would be nearly halfway to zenith, and its globe would have 6,390 times the area of the moon as we see it from Earth's surface.

Since Saturn is 9.5 times as far from the sun as the moon is, it receives only $\frac{1}{90}$ as much light per unit area. On the other hand, Saturn reflects seven times as large a fraction of the light it does receive as the moon does. Combining these two facts, we see that a given area of Saturn's disc, as seen from a satellite, gleams with only $\frac{1}{13}$ the light of the same area of the moon as seen from Earth. As a result, when fully illuminated Saturn delivers only 492 times as much light to Janus as the moon does to Earth.

This is not quite a record for a satellite. From Jupiter's innermost satellite, Amalthea, Jupiter has an apparent width of 46 degrees and shines with a light, when full, equal to 1,200 times that of the full moon. From Mars's inner satellite, Mars appears slightly smaller than Saturn does to Janus, but Mars, being closer to the sun, is more brightly illuminated than either Jupiter or Saturn, and when full delivers 5,700 times as much light to its inner satellite as does the full moon to us.

Yet suppose we were on a particle on the inner edge of Saturn's rings, whirling about Saturn every six hours. From that vantage point Saturn would stretch across a width of 76.1 degrees, filling one sixth of the entire sky. It would have 21,600 times the area of our moon as we see it, and would shine with a light equal to 1,700 times that of our full moon. That would certainly outdo Jupiter as seen from Amalthea in both size and brightness; and Mars as seen from Phobos in size, if not in brightness.

Since, very likely, the satellites of Saturn (with the possible exception of Phoebe) present the same side to the planet as they revolve about it (just as the moon does to us), Saturn is fixed to its position in their sky. From one hemisphere of the satellite, Saturn is always in the sky, its exact position depending on where in that hemisphere you are standing. From the other hemisphere, Saturn is never in the sky, just as the Earth cannot be seen from the far side of the moon.

For each satellite, the sun seems to circle the sky once in every revolution about Saturn, so that the period of revolution is also the length of that satellite's day. On Janus, the sun races from rising to setting in seven and a half hours, and on Iapetus, the sun remains in the sky between rising and setting some forty Earth days.

Although the sun is so shrunken at the distance of Saturn as not really to show a disc, it still shines with a light equal to 5,200 times the brightness of our full moon. That means that even from the innermost particles of the rings, the sun yields three times as much light as swollen Saturn does.

Naturally, if we are on the hemisphere of a satellite where Saturn is never in sight, the sun is unrivaled when it crosses the sky. When standing on the hemisphere from which we see Saturn, the planet is in its full phase when the sun is on the other side of the satellite and it is Saturn that is then unrivaled.

When the sun rises, Saturn is only half illuminated, and the higher the sun rises in the sky, the less of Saturn is illuminated.

From the nearest satellites—Janus, Mimas, and Enceladus— the sun moves into eclipse by Saturn every time it crosses the sky. During the eclipse it is the far side of Saturn that gets the sun, so that from the satellite we see Saturn as a dark circle in the sky, only visible because it obscures the stars behind it.

Sunlight, gleaming through the upper atmosphere on every side of Saturn, will produce a pale illumination, a glowing ring in the sky that will also mark the position of Saturn.

Because the axis of Saturn (and the orbits of the inner satellites) is tipped by 26 degrees to its plane of revolution around the sun, the sun crosses the satellite sky at different heights, depending on the position of Saturn in its orbit. When the sun moves behind Saturn in such a way as to cross its maximum width, the eclipse is longest and the ring of light is equally bright all around at the middle of the eclipse. When the sun moves behind Saturn, above or below its center, the eclipse is shorter in duration and the ring of light is always lopsided.

From Tethys outward, Saturn appears sufficiently small so that the sun, in crossing the sky, may miss the planet altogether at times, and there is then no eclipse. On Titan, for instance, the sun crosses the sky twenty-three times each Earth year, and there is an eclipse on only four or five of those occasions.

From any one of the satellites, one or more of the other satellites would be present in the sky, and of them all, Titan would make the best sight since, after all, it is the largest and brightest of Saturn's satellites.

Hyperion approaches more closely to Titan than does any other satellite, the distance between them being as small as 261,000 kilometers (162,000 miles) when both are in a straight line with Saturn. At such a time, Titan as seen from Hyperion has a diameter of 1.27 degrees and an area six times that of the full moon as seen by us.

In the faint sunlight of the Saturnian system, Titan would only deliver half the light to Hyperion that the moon does to us, but it would shine with a very beautiful orange light just the same.

If we were standing on the hemisphere of Hyperion facing Saturn, Titan would be at its largest as it moved between

Hyperion and Saturn. This would happen every 63.6 days. Titan's apparent width would then be nearly one third that of Saturn as seen from Hyperion. As Titan passed before Saturn, both bodies would always be in the same phase and one could view the passage in different forms—both would be full, or half, or crescent, or anything in between.

There would be no satellite-Saturn combination as impressive seen from any other vantage point in the Saturnian system, and if we could imagine the satellites as tourist spots, Titan would be Hyperion's selling point, as Saturn would be Janus's.

The greatest attraction of all would, however, be invisible from eight of the satellites. From Janus to Hyperion, the satellites revolve in a plane very little removed from that of the rings. That means that from those satellites, the rings would always be seen almost or entirely edge-on. They could never be seen as anything but, at best, a thin bright line crossing Saturn and extending outward on either side. Even that would be exceptional.

Iapetus, however, revolves in a plane that is tipped 15 degrees to that of the rings. This means that watching Saturn in the course of a single revolution of Iapetus, we would see the rings first, let us say, at the invisible stage when Iapetus crosses Saturn's equatorial plane. As Iapetus rose above Saturn's equatorial plane, we would see more and more of the top surface of the rings. To the observer on Iapetus, it would seem that Saturn and its rings were tipping downward more and more.

Eventually there would be a maximum downward tip. Saturn and its rings would slowly tip upward again until finally the rings would disappear. Then they would reappear and this time we would see the lower side. Again a maximum is reached and then Saturn rights itself a second time, as Iapetus's revolution is completed. The whole thing then repeats.

This is exactly what happens when Saturn and its rings are viewed from Earth. On Earth the complete cycle takes thirty years, but on Iapetus it takes just under eighty days. Further, from Earth the spectacle is visible only in a good telescope, while on Iapetus it would, of course, be visible to the naked eye, since Saturn would be as bright as the moon appears to us and would be fourteen times as large.

Since the rings reflect more light than Saturn itself does, Saturn would become brighter in the sky as it tipped and would be brightest at maximum tip. Naturally, depending on where the sun was in the sky, different parts of the ring system would be in sunlight and different parts in Saturn's night shadow. A crescent Saturn, with the rings extending some distance across the dark part of the sphere before being cut off by the night shadow, would be particularly spectacular. Surely the rings would be Iapetus's claim to being a tourist attraction.

About the only way in which the view from Iapetus is inferior to that from Earth is that as seen from Earth, Saturn tips twice as far downward and upward, at maximum, as it does when seen from Iapetus.

From Phoebe the tip of Saturn and its rings is greater than from Iapetus and even very slightly greater than from Earth. From Phoebe, however, Saturn and its rings are considerably smaller than as seen from Iapetus—no larger than the moon appears to us. Furthermore, the rate of tipping back and forth is slower, so that maximum tip (that would presumably mark the height of the tourist season) comes every 270 days on Phoebe as compared with every 40 days on Iapetus.

Any talk of the Saturnian satellites as tourist attractions is, of course, science fiction and is not meant seriously (at least not now). In some ways, though, one can more easily talk about Saturn's satellites than those of Jupiter in connection with tourism.

Saturn is twice as far away from us as Jupiter, but Saturn may not be as dangerous. Jupiter is known to have an enormous magnetic field that traps charged particles. Jupiter's large satellites whirl through this magnetic field and manned spaceships may not be able to approach them because of the radiation danger.

As yet, we don't know the nature of Saturn's magnetic field. It very likely has one, but the magnetic field should be less intense than Jupiter's, since Saturn is less massive and spins a little more slowly. Then, too, Saturn is twice as far from the sun as Jupiter is and it is the sun that is the source of charged particles.

It may be, then, that the neighborhood of Saturn offers less trouble from the radiation point of view than that of Jupiter. Also, Saturn's gravitational field is less intense and, therefore, less dangerous than Jupiter's. On both counts, then, it is conceivable that human beings may approach Saturn's chief satellites before they dare approach those of Jupiter.

### The Size of Saturn's Satellites

The order in which Saturn's satellites were discovered is roughly that of their apparent brightness. Naturally, the brighter they are, the easier they are to see and, therefore, to discover. The one other point to remember is that if two satellites are of equal brightness, the one farther from Saturn is likely to be discovered first since its light is less likely to be obscured by Saturn's greater brightness (see Table 46).

As soon as Cassini had discovered the second of Saturn's satellites, Iapetus, it was clear that something new had been found. Up to that point, six satellites were known and all were three to six thousand kilometers in diameter. That might well have seemed a natural size for satellites, and one might suppose that all satellites had to be that size.

That would be wrong, of course. Naturally, the large satellites would catch and reflect more light and would be the first

# TABLE 46

## Brightness of Saturn's Satellites

| SATELLITE | ORDER OF DISCOVERY | MAXIMUM BRIGHTNESS (MAGNITUDE) |
|---|---|---|
| Janus | 10 | 14 |
| Mimas | 7 | 12.2 |
| Enceladus | 6 | 11.8 |
| Tethys | 5 | 10.5 |
| Dione | 4 | 10.6 |
| Rhea | 3 | 9.9 |
| Titan | 1 | 8.3 |
| Hyperion | 8 | 14 |
| Iapetus | 2 | 10.7 |
| Phoebe | 9 | 15 |

to be discovered.* Once those were all found, then the satellites discovered later, as telescopes improved, would have to be smaller (except for large ones that were very dim because they were exceedingly far away).

Iapetus was so much dimmer than Titan, however, even though both objects were about equally far from Earth, that it seemed clear that Iapetus must be considerably smaller. In fact, it was less than two thousand kilometers in diameter and this was also true of all the other Saturnian satellites found later.

In Table 47 the diameters of the various Saturnian satellites are given, with the warning that, except for Titan, the figures are somewhat uncertain and are almost sure to be modified once we get the proper information from the Saturn probes.

---

* Our moon, of course, would have been seen first even if it were quite small since it is so close to us. It is pure chance that it happened to be a large satellite, and that Earth had no small one.

# TABLE 47

## Diameters of Saturn's Satellites

| SATELLITE | KILOMETERS | MILES |
|---|---|---|
| Janus | 300 | 200 |
| Mimas | 400 | 250 |
| Enceladus | 600 | 375 |
| Tethys | 1,000 | 625 |
| Dione | 800 | 500 |
| Rhea | 1,600 | 1,000 |
| Titan | 5,800 | 3,600 |
| Hyperion | 440 | 275 |
| Iapetus | 1,600 | 1,000 |
| Phoebe | 240 | 150 |

When Iapetus was discovered in 1671, it was the smallest astronomical body that had yet been found, breaking the record which Europa had set in 1610. Dione broke the record again in 1684; then Enceladus, and then Mimas, broke it in 1789.

Titan's large size does not show up sufficiently if we just consider diameters. Volume varies as the cube of the diameter. If, then, Titan's diameter is 3⅝ times that of Rhea or Iapetus, the next largest satellites, its volume is 3⅝ × 3⅝ × 3⅝, or 47.6 times greater than either of those. In fact, Titan's volume is twenty times that of all the remaining nine satellites put together.

This emphasizes the fact that of all Saturn's satellites, only one, Titan, is really sizable, so that when the ten satellites are viewed from Saturn's "surface," they don't make as brave a showing as one might expect (see Table 48).

# TABLE 48

## Apparent Diameters of Saturn's Satellites

| SATELLITE | MINUTES OF ARC | MOON AS SEEN FROM EARTH = 1 |
|---|---|---|
| Janus | 6.3 | 0.20 |
| Mimas | 7.1 | 0.23 |
| Enceladus | 8.4 | 0.27 |
| Tethys | 12.0 | 0.39 |
| Dione | 7.0 | 0.22 |
| Rhea | 11.1 | 0.36 |
| Titan | 16.5 | 0.53 |
| Hyperion | 1.0 | 0.03 |
| Iapetus | 1.5 | 0.05 |
| Phoebe | 0.06 | 0.002 |

Hyperion and Iapetus would merely have the appearance of fairly bright stars in Saturn's sky, while Phoebe would be invisible to the unaided eye. Of the rest, Janus, Mimas, Enceladus, and Dione would be just barely large enough to look like tiny marbles. Only Tethys, Rhea, and Titan would look like distinct orbs and show clear phases, though each would appear considerably smaller than our moon does to us.

The apparent area of all ten satellites as seen from Saturn's "surface" is only about three fourths the area of our moon as seen from Earth's surface. The brightness of all ten satellites as seen from Saturn would certainly be less than one third the brightness of our single full moon. Of course, the changing pattern of the satellites in Saturn's sky would be full of interest even if none of them was very impressive singly.

And yet we mustn't overemphasize the smallness of Saturn's

satellites, either. Of the known Saturnian satellites, Phoebe, with a diameter of 240 kilometers (150 miles), is the smallest. Yet of Jupiter's satellites, only the four large satellites, which have diameters ranging from 3,060 to 5,220 kilometers (1,900 to 3,240 miles; see Table 32), are clearly larger than that, and Amalthea may be only as large as Phoebe. All the other satellites of Jupiter are considerably smaller than either Phoebe or Amalthea.

Suppose we were to decide, arbitrarily, that we were only going to count those satellites which were at least 200 kilometers (125 miles) in diameter, and that anything less would just be circling fragments of no importance. In that case it would turn out that Mercury, Venus, and Mars would have no satellites, Earth would have one, and Jupiter would have five. Saturn, however, would have ten and be far in the lead.

In fact, we should perhaps count Saturn as having eleven, for if all the matter in the rings were put together, they would form a satellite larger than any of Saturn's satellites but Titan.

The masses of the satellites (see Table 49) are, except for that of Titan, even more uncertain than the diameters, and could be subject to considerable change once the probes send back the proper data.

Each satellite, having mass, also has a small gravitational field which can evidence itself as a surface gravity (see Table 50).

A human being who weighed 70 kilograms (154 pounds) on Earth and, therefore, 11.7 kilograms (25.7 pounds) on the moon would weigh 7.8 kilograms (17.2 pounds) on Titan and only 0.24 kilograms (0.52 pounds) on Phoebe.

It wouldn't seem that the gravitational pull of the smaller satellites of Saturn would have much of an effect, but there is one thing that pull does that is visible from Earth.

Let us go back to Cassini's Division.

# TABLE 49

## Masses of Saturn's Satellites

| SATELLITE | MASS (MOON = 1) |
|---|---|
| Rings | 0.33 |
| Janus | 0.0002 |
| Mimas | 0.0005 |
| Enceladus | 0.0010 |
| Tethys | 0.0085 |
| Dione | 0.0158 |
| Rhea | 0.025 |
| Titan | 1.905 |
| Hyperion | 0.0015 |
| Iapetus | 0.020 |
| Phoebe | 0.0001 |

If there were ring fragments in that gap, they would circle Saturn in 11.4 to 11.8 hours, depending on where in the gap they were. Compare this with the periods of revolution of the inner satellites as in Table 51.

Now imagine a particle in Cassini's Division, with Janus and Mimas in a line directly away from Saturn. The particle in Cassini's Division, moving faster than the two satellites, would pull away and the gravitational pull of those satellites would drag it back. Other particles approaching that point would be pulled forward by the satellites.

Every time the particle circled Saturn twice, Mimas would have circled it once and would be pulling back at the particle again, or forward, exactly as before. Every time the particles circled Saturn three times, Janus would have circled it twice

# TABLE 50

## Surface Gravity of Saturn's Satellites

| | SURFACE GRAVITY | |
|---|---|---|
| SATELLITE | EARTH = 1 | MOON = 1 |
| Janus | 0.0044 | 0.026 |
| Mimas | 0.0062 | 0.037 |
| Enceladus | 0.0054 | 0.033 |
| Tethys | 0.016 | 0.10 |
| Dione | 0.048 | 0.29 |
| Rhea | 0.019 | 0.12 |
| Titan | 0.111 | 0.67 |
| Hyperion | 0.015 | 0.092 |
| Iapetus | 0.015 | 0.092 |
| Phoebe | 0.0034 | 0.020 |

# TABLE 51

## Cassini's Division

| | PERIOD OF REVOLUTION | |
|---|---|---|
| SATELLITES | HOURS | CASSINI'S GAP = 1 |
| Cassini's Division | 11.5 | 1.00 |
| Janus | 17.98 | 1.56 |
| Mimas | 22.61 | 1.97 |

and would be back in place exerting its pull. Every time the particles circled Saturn six times, Janus would have circled it four times and Mimas three times and both would be renewing their pull.

Over and over, the same pull would be exerted, either always forward for some particles, or always backward for other particles. In the end, some particles would be pulled forward into a wider orbit around Saturn, and others would be pulled backward into a narrower orbit. They would either move farther from Saturn or drop in closer; they would *not* stay in Cassini's Division.

Elsewhere in the rings, particles would not circle in such convenient exact fractions of the periods of revolution of nearby satellites and no important changes would be produced. That is why only Cassini's gap is cleared so efficiently, and so is the only wide division in the rings.

If we know the mass and volume of each of Saturn's satellites, we can calculate the density. With the mass and volume for most of them both quite uncertain, the value of the density is more uncertain still and Table 52 must be accepted with great caution.

Still, if these are accepted as the best figures we have at the moment, it would seem that Dione is a rocky satellite, like our Moon or Io. Hyperion is a mixture of rock and ices, while the rest are apparently mixtures of various ices. Saturn's rings, from their brightness, would also seem to be made up largely of ice; in all likelihood, of water ice.

In this respect, Iapetus is particularly interesting. When Cassini first discovered it in 1671, he noticed that it was about five times as bright when it was to the west of Saturn as when it was to the east. Since Iapetus probably always keeps one face turned toward Saturn, we see one hemisphere when it is on one side of Saturn and the other hemisphere when it is on the other side.

# TABLE 52

## Densities of Saturn's Satellites

| SATELLITE | DENSITY (WATER ICE = 1) |
|---|---|
| Janus | 1.2 |
| Mimas | 1.2 |
| Enceladus | 0.8 |
| Tethys | 1.3 |
| Dione | 4.8 |
| Rhea | 1.0 |
| Titan | 1.5 |
| Hyperion | 2.7 |
| Iapetus | 0.8 |
| Phoebe | 1.1 |

Apparently, one hemisphere of Iapetus happens to reflect sunlight five times as efficiently as the other. One side may have ice on its surface while the other side is bare rock. If so, it is easier to assume that Iapetus is essentially rocky with a thin layer of ice on the surface of one hemisphere, rather than that it is essentially icy with a thin layer of rock on the surface of one hemisphere. If that is the case, the density given in the table for Iapetus must be quite wrong. The Saturn probes may conceivably give us information on this subject.

# 6

## COMETS AND ASTEROIDS

### *Halley's Comet and Others*

The ancient Greeks thought Saturn was the farthest planet. So did Copernicus and Galileo. Right up to 1700, it was somehow taken for granted that Saturn's orbit was the boundary of the solar system and that nothing went beyond it.

The first object that broke through that boundary and freed astronomers from the notion of a Saturnian limit to the solar system was a comet.

Comets have been known since prehistoric times, for a bright one is very noticeable when it is in the sky. They are very puzzling, too, for they are like nothing else in the sky. They are fuzzy, cloudy patches of light, with irregular shapes. Usually they have streamers of light that some people imagine look like hair. The very word "comet" is from a Latin word for "hair." Furthermore, comets come and go unpredictably and don't seem to have the regular motions other astronomical objects have.

The Greek philosopher Aristotle (AR-is-tot-l, 384 B.C.–322 B.C.) suggested that these puzzles could be solved by supposing that comets were not astronomical bodies at all but were regions of burning vapors in the upper atmosphere.

Most people in early times, even astronomers, were certain

that comets were objects of ill omen, sent to announce catastrophes. They therefore spent their time trying to work out what the coming catastrophes might be rather than taking the trouble to observe the comet carefully.

The first astronomer who made the effort to observe a comet carefully enough to mark its position in the sky together with the changes in that position from night to night was the German astronomer Regiomontanus (ray-jee-oh-mon-TAY nus, 1436–1476). He did this for a bright comet that appeared in 1472.

In 1531 an Italian observer, Girolamo Fracastoro (fra-kas-TOH-roh, 1483–1553), studied a comet that appeared that year, and in 1538 pointed out that the streamers of a comet (usually called a "tail") always pointed away from the sun. That seemed a point against Aristotle's theory and in favor of some connection between comets and the sun.

The Danish astronomer Tycho Brahe (TY-koh-BRAH-uh, 1546–1601) tried to measure the parallax of a comet that appeared in 1577. He failed, because the parallax turned out to be smaller than that of the moon and too small to measure without a telescope (which hadn't yet been invented). That meant the comet was more distant than the moon and was an astronomical body and not an atmospheric phenomenon.

After Kepler had worked out the elliptical orbits of the planets, the question arose as to whether comets might have elliptical orbits too. The Italian astronomer Giovanni Alfonso Borelli (boh-REL-lee, 1608–1679) studied a comet that appeared in the sky in 1664 and suggested that it followed a path around the sun that was like an ellipse that was so long that the other end never closed. Such a long, non-closing curve is called a parabola. If comets had parabolic orbits, then each comet would enter the solar system from some far-off reach of the universe, become visible when it was close enough to the sun, move around the sun, and then depart forever.

The English astronomer Edmund Halley (HAL-lee, 1656–1742) carefully studied a comet that appeared in 1682. He traced its path across the sky and noted that it followed the same path that Fracastoro's comet of 1531 had taken. There had also been comets in 1456 and 1607 that had been reported in the same parts of the sky. It could be that comets did return and that all these were one, which returned every seventy-five or seventy-six years.

Using the data, and the law of gravitation which had just been worked out by Isaac Newton, Halley worked out an elliptical orbit for the comet, and in 1705 predicted it would return in 1758. Halley did not live to see it, but the comet did return and has been known as Halley's comet ever since.

For the first time a comet's orbit had been worked out, and a comet had been shown to be an orderly part of the solar system.

The orbit was a long and very eccentric ellipse.

At perihelion (when it is nearest the sun), Halley's comet is 87,800,000 kilometers (54,600,000 miles) from the sun. It is then between the orbits of Venus and Mercury.

Because the eccentricity is 0.967, however, Halley's comet is very far from the sun at aphelion (when it is at the point in its orbit that is farthest from the sun). It recedes to a distance of 5,240,000,000 kilometers (3,250,000,000 miles) from the sun. This is no less than 3.67 times as far from the sun as Saturn is. That really breaks the notion of a Saturnian boundary to the solar system. Halley's comet makes Saturn look like a neighbor of the sun (see Figure 16).

Since Halley's time, the orbits of about forty-five other comets have been calculated, almost all of them with periods less than that of Halley's. The comet with the shortest-known period is Encke's comet, named for the German astronomer Johann Franz Encke (ENK-uh, 1791–1865). Its period is 3.30 years. At perihelion it is only 51,600,000 kilometers (31,400,000 miles)

Fig. 16—Halley's Comet

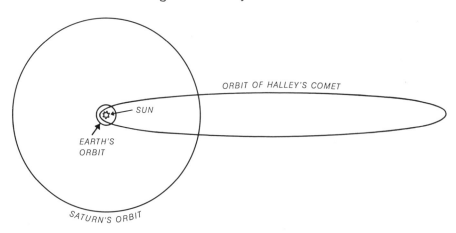

from the sun and it is then a little closer to the sun than Mercury is. At aphelion, it is 611,000,000 kilometers (380,000,000 miles) from the sun.

Even at its farthest, Encke's comet doesn't recede from the sun as far as Jupiter's orbit. It is the only known comet whose orbit fits inside Jupiter's.

The comet with an established period that is longest is Rigollet's comet, which at perihelion is 112,000,000 kilometers (69,500,000 miles) from the sun. It is then just a little farther from the sun than Venus is. Its orbit has an eccentricity of 0.974, however, so that Rigollet's comet recedes at aphelion to a distance of 8,500,000,000 kilometers (5,300,000,000 miles) from the sun. This is six times as far from the sun as Saturn is and 1.6 times as far as Halley's comet ever gets. Rigollet's comet returns only every 156 years.

Comets consist largely of icy materials, as was suggested in 1949 by the American astronomer Fred Lawrence Whipple (1906–    ). As long as they are far away from the sun and beyond the orbit of Jupiter, the ices of which they are composed are frozen hard and hold together.

When comets move in toward the sun, however, the sun's heat vaporizes the icy materials and liberates small grains of rocky and metallic substances that may also be present. The still frozen kernel of the comet (the "nucleus") is then surrounded by a haze of dust and vapor which is the "coma."

Emerging from the sun there is a constant stream of speeding subatomic particles moving outward in all directions. This was named the "solar wind" in 1958 by the American scientist Eugene Newman Parker (1927–    ). The solar wind sweeps the dust and gas of the coma into streamers pointing away from the sun, thus forming the comet's tail.

Because of the solar wind, some of the cometary material is lost each time the comet moves through perihelion. With each appearance, a comet grows less bright and spectacular. In the end, all or almost all its ice is gone and left behind is only a small kernel of rock and metal, or else nothing but a cloud of rock and metal dust that spreads all through the comet's orbit.

For this reason, periodic comets are rarely spectacular. Encke's comet, for instance, can be spotted only in a good telescope and it shows only the smallest possible haze to mark it as a comet. It is virtually nothing but solid nucleus.

Halley's comet is still bright because it approaches the sun only once every seventy-six years, so it hasn't lost as much of its icy material as it would have if it had a shorter period. Even so, its last appearance in 1910 was not very spectacular and its next appearance in 1986 probably won't be.

There are comets with periods much longer even than that of Rigollet's comet, comets which have such elongated orbits that they can't be calculated exactly. Astronomers can only say that those comets follow such enormous ellipses that they return to the sun only after intervals of hundreds of thousands, or even millions, of years. They have lost virtually none of their icy materials and when they do show up they can be spectacular indeed. There were a number of such comets in the 1800s, but, as luck would have it, not one has been seen in the 1900s that has been a real blazer.

About 500 of these long-period comets have been reported in history. The Dutch astronomer Jan Hendrik Oort (AWRT, 1900–    ) suggested in 1950 that there was a belt of comets circling the sun very slowly, at a distance of several trillion kilometers. Bilions of small bits of icy material, several kilometers across, might exist there; left over, perhaps, from when the original cloud of dust and gas contracted to form the sun and the planets.

Every once in a while the gravitational influence of a nearby star might pull one of those very distant comets ahead in its orbit and cause it to move farther out from the sun. It might even be lost to the solar system altogether and go wandering off independently in the enormous spaces between the stars.

Then, too, the gravitational influence of a nearby star might pull back on a comet and cause it to drop inward toward the neighborhood of the sun, thus starting a process that will end in its death. The gravitational influence of the planets may alter its orbit into a short one so that it approaches the sun every century or less and then the process of disintegration and death is hastened greatly.

Recently, comets that are far enough from the sun to remain hard and to show no signs of surrounding dust or vapor have come to be called "cometoids." Oort's suggestion, then, is of a belt of cometoids, and every comet that glows hazily when it approaches the sun becomes a hard and solid cometoid when it is far from the sun.

Though comets are very noticeable objects when near the sun, they are so small that as cometoids they are undetectable once they move into the farther reaches of their orbits.

In 1973, for instance, a comet was detected by the Czech astronomer Lubos Kohoutek, at a distance of 778,000,000 kilometers (483,000,000 miles) from the sun. This is just about at the distance of Jupiter's orbit, and to see one at that distance was very unusual. For that reason it was assumed that "Kohoutek's comet" was a large one that had not been in the vicinity of the sun many times, or that was perhaps approaching it for the first time. It was hoped that it would prove a great spectacle. Unfortunately, the comet could not have been very icy, but must have been rather rocky so that while useful to scientists, it did not put in much of a display for the unaided eye.

Every comet ever seen by an astronomer has had its perihelion quite close to the sun. The comet with the farthest known perihelion is Schwassman-Wachmann's comet which, at perihelion, is 826,000,000 kilometers (513,000,000 miles) from the sun. This is just beyond Jupiter's orbit, but its orbit is not very elliptical, having an eccentricity of only 0.136. At aphelion, therefore, its distance is only 1,086,000,000 kilometers (675,000,000 miles), which is closer than the orbit of Saturn. Schwassman-Wachmann's comet has an orbit, in short, that lies between those of Jupiter and Saturn at every point.

To summarize, then, every comet that has ever been seen has had the visible part of its orbit inside the orbit of Saturn. Though it is quite likely that there are vast numbers of comets with orbits lying far outside that of Saturn at every point, these have never been seen.

As far as comets are concerned, therefore, Saturn is still the visible limit of the solar system.

## *From Icarus to Hidalgo*

Comets are not the only small bodies of the solar system.

An Italian astronomer, Giuseppe Piazzi (PYAH-tzee), was engaged in correcting a star map as the year 1800 was drawing to a close.

After midnight on New Year's Eve, therefore on January 1, 1801, the first night of the nineteenth century, he noted a star in the constellation Taurus that was not on the map at all. He checked its position the next night and found it had moved. The night after, it had moved again. It was not a star at all, but an object that was moving around the sun.

At first Piazzi thought it was a comet, though it showed no haze but appeared as a sharp point, like a star. When its orbit was calculated by a German mathematician, Johann Karl Friedrich Gauss (GOWS, 1777–1855), that orbit turned out to be only very slightly elliptical and to lie entirely between the orbits of Mars and Jupiter. Its average distance from the sun turned out to be 413,800,000 kilometers (257,100,000 miles).

Piazzi named the new object Ceres (SEE-reez), for the Roman goddess of agriculture, who was particularly associated with his home island of Sicily.

Ceres's motions were exactly like those expected of a planet, but it was surprisingly dim, not quite bright enough to be seen without a telescope. To be that dim when it was less than half as far from Earth as Jupiter was, it would have to be very small —and it is. The diameter of Ceres is 1,070 kilometers (660 miles). It has only $\frac{1}{280}$ the mass of Mercury, the smallest planet known up to that point, and only $\frac{1}{62}$ the mass of our moon.

Certain astronomers had come to the conclusion, a few years earlier, that there might be a small planet between the orbits of Mars and Jupiter.* They had just begun a program for finding it when the news of the discovery of Ceres came through.

---

* I'll explain the reasons they thought so later in the book.

They continued the program anyway, feeling that Ceres was so small that it might not represent all the planetary material in that part of the solar system.

They were right. By 1807 three more planets, each even smaller than Ceres, were discovered, and all of them had orbits that lay btween those of Mars and Jupiter.

These planets were so small that even through the telescope they did not expand into globes but remained, in appearance, starlike points of light. It became customary, therefore, to call them "asteroids" from Greek words meaning "starlike."

More and more asteroids were discovered as the nineteenth century wore on, especially after photography came to be used to help find them, and by 1900 well over four hundred asteroids were known with orbits that lay between those of Mars and Jupiter. This region was called the "asteroid belt."

Do any asteroids exist outside the asteroid belt? The answer is, yes.

On August 13, 1898, the German astronomer Gustav Witt (VIT) discovered Asteroid #433. When its orbit was calculated it turned out that during part of its travel about the sun it moved inward, out of the asteroid belt and past the orbit of Mars. At perihelion, #433 is only 170,000,000 kilometers (106,-000,000 miles) from the sun. It approaches the sun almost as closely as Earth does.

Until then, all the asteroids had been given feminine names in accordance with the precedent set by the use of the name Ceres. Witt, however, gave #433 the name of Eros (EE-ros), the Greek god of love. From then on, asteroids with orbits that took them outside the asteroid belt for at least part of their journey about the sun have been given masculine names.

Since the discovery of Eros, other asteroids have been found that ventured inside Mars's orbit. In 1948 the German-American astronomer Walter Baade (BAH-duh, 1893–1960) discovered Asteroid #1566. It turned out to come closer to the sun than any other asteroid. At perihelion, it is only 28,500,000 kilometers (17,700,000 miles) from the sun, so it approaches the sun considerably closer than even Mercury does. Its orbital eccentricity, however, is 0.83, so at aphelion it is 307,000,000 kilometers (191,000,000 miles) from the sun and it is then well within the asteroid belt.

Baade named this asteroid Icarus, for the young man in the Greek myths who flew through the air on artificial wings in which the feathers were fixed to the frame by wax. He flew too near the sun, the wax melted, and he fell to his death.

All the asteroids that move out of the asteroid belt and approach the sun more closely at perihelion than Mars does remain in the belt at the aphelion end of their orbits. It is possible, though, that these inward-moving asteroids might move close enough to some planet to be captured and to become satellites of that planet. The two small satellites of Mars are thought to be captured asteroids.

What about asteroids that move out of the belt in the other direction, past the orbit of Jupiter?

If these exist, they would be more difficult to discover. The outer boundary of the asteroid belt is about eight times as far away from Earth as the inner boundary. Small asteroids easily visible at the inner boundary would be very difficult to see at the outer boundary. Some of the asteroids that venture inside the orbit of Mars are only a couple of kilometers across and can be detected. Asteroids at the outer boundary of the asteroid belt would have to be at least 50 kilometers across to be made out easily.

In 1906 a German astronomer, Max Wolf, discovered Asteroid #588. It was unusual because it moved at a surprisingly slow speed and therefore had to be unusually far from the sun. It was, up to that point, the farthest asteroid that had ever been discovered.

Its orbit was sufficiently unusual for Wolf to decide to give it a masculine name. He called it Achilles after the hero of the Greek forces in the Trojan War.

Once the orbit of Achilles was worked out, it was found to be traveling in Jupiter's orbit, in a position about 60 degrees ahead of Jupiter and staying in that position as both turned about the sun. The sun, Jupiter, and Achilles were so placed that if imaginary lines were drawn from the sun to Jupiter to Achilles and back to the sun, an equilateral triangle would be formed.

Back in 1772, the Italian-French astronomer Joseph Louis Lagrange (lah-GRAHNZH, 1736–1813) had shown that from gravitational theory such an equilateral triangle arrangement was stable and all three bodies would keep their positions, provided that the largest body was at least twenty-five times as massive as the second largest, and that the smallest body was very small.

But we can draw another equilateral triangle with one of the angles in Jupiter's orbit 60 degrees behind Jupiter. Within months after the discovery of Achilles, an asteroid was located in that position too. It was Asteroid #617 and it was named Patroclus after Achilles's friend in Homer's tale of the Trojan War (see Figure 17).

Because of these names, the asteroids located in these triangular positions are called "Trojan asteroids." They are located in the "Trojan positions."

Astronomers realized at once that it was very likely that more than one asteroid might be in each of the Trojan positions and, indeed, others were found.

About fifteen asteroids have been spotted in the neighborhood of Achilles and five in the neighborhood of Patroclus and all have been given the names of warriors taking part in the Trojan War. Some astronomers estimate that there are seven hundred or more Trojan asteroids altogether, but naturally we see only the largest.

Fig. 17—The Trojan Asteroids

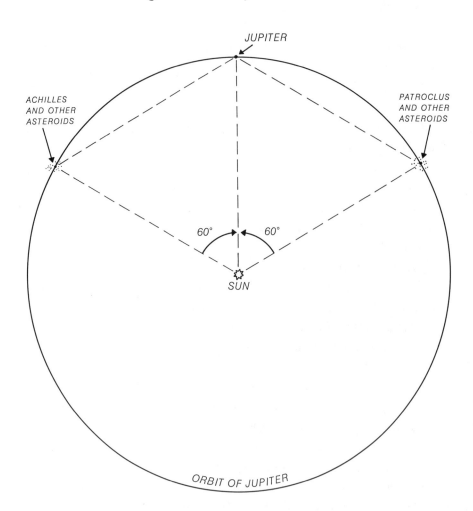

JUPITER

ACHILLES
AND OTHER
ASTEROIDS

PATROCLUS
AND OTHER
ASTEROIDS

60°   60°

SUN

ORBIT OF JUPITER

The Trojan asteroids do not remain exactly in the Trojan positions. They would, if the sun, Jupiter, and they were the only bodies in existence. The other planets, however, particularly Saturn, do exert a gravitational influence and this causes each to oscillate about the Trojan position as they move about the sun.

The oscillations can be wide indeed and a Trojan asteroid can venture tens of millions of kilometers from the Trojan position. It is possible that a combination of gravitational pulls can occasionally cause one to wander so far off that it moves away permanently and ceases to be a Trojan asteroid. Other asteroids, of course, may happen to move closely enough to the Trojan position to be trapped, so that through the history of the solar system there probably have always been a large number of asteroids in both positions, although the stay of any one particular asteroid may not be very long.

It is possible that an asteroid lost from one of the Trojan positions might eventually venture so close to Jupiter itself as to be trapped in orbit about that giant planet. In fact, the eight or nine small satellites circling Jupiter beyond the orbit of Callisto are all thought to be captured asteroids—possibly Trojans, though not necessarily.

It is also possible that a Trojan asteroid on losing its place might do so in an outward direction and might, so to speak, be hurled beyond Jupiter.

In 1920 Walter Baade (who, over a quarter of a century later, was to discover Icarus) discovered Asteroid #944, which he called Hidalgo (hih-DAL-goh). This is not a mythological name but is what Spaniards call a nobleman of the lower ranks. When its orbit was calcuated it was found that Hidalgo moved outward far beyond Jupiter and has an orbital period of 13.7 years, three times that of the average asteroid and even longer than that of Jupiter. It could be an ejected Trojan asteroid, but it would be very difficult to prove that.

Hidalgo has a high orbital eccentricity of 0.66, the highest of any known asteroid except Icarus. At perihelion it is only about 300,000,000 kilometers (190,000,000 miles) from the sun, so that in that point of its orbit it is neatly within the asteroid belt. At aphelion, however, it is 1,450,000,000 kilometers (895,-000,000 miles) away from the sun, or just about as far from the sun as Saturn is (see Figure 18).

Fig. 18—Hidalgo

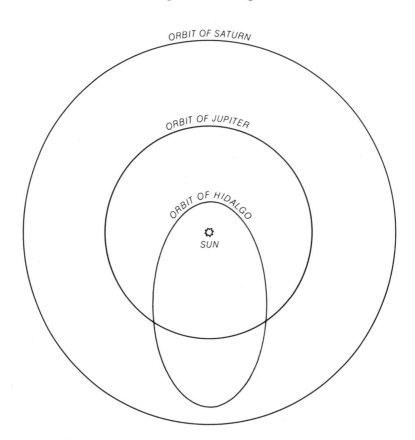

ORBIT OF SATURN

ORBIT OF JUPITER

ORBIT OF HIDALGO

☼
SUN

From Figure 18 it might seem that Hidalgo approaches so close to Saturn that it is in danger of capture, but the figure is only two-dimensional. Hidalgo's orbital inclination is 43 degrees, so that it moves slantwise with respect to Saturn. At aphelion it is so far below Saturn as to be no closer to that planet than Earth is.

## *Chiron*

Until the 1970s all asteroids which had been discovered, no matter how unusual their orbits, were still members of the asteroid belt at least part of the time. Asteroids like Eros and Icarus, which were inside the asteroid belt at perihelion, were in the asteroid belt at aphelion. Asteroids like Hidalgo, which were outside the asteroid belt at aphelion, were in the asteroid belt at perihelion.

Are there asteroids, however, that remain inside Mars's orbit at all times?

In 1977 the American astronomer Charles Kowall found a small asteroid whose orbit is closer to the sun than Mars at all points, but which remains always farther from the sun than the orbit of Venus. Its average distance from the sun is not very much different from that of Earth.

In this book, however, we are more interested in the distant regions of the solar system than the nearby ones. Are there asteroids whose orbit lies outside the orbit of Jupiter at every point? If there were, they would be very difficult to find. In the first place, even a large asteroid would look dim indeed in positions beyond Jupiter. In the second place, it would be moving at slow speeds (the farther from the sun, the more slowly an orbiting object moves) and the slow change in position might be overlooked.

Throughout 1977, however, Kowall was studying the sky with particular attention to very slow-moving objects that might lie beyond Jupiter. He was looking particularly for distant comets. While he was making the search, he located a few comets that were not particularly distant, and also the asteroid that remained inside Mars's orbit at all times.

Then, on November 1, 1977, came a more interesting discovery.

Kowall detected a speck of light that was very dim, with a magnitude of only 18, and that was moving at only one third the speed of Jupiter. It therefore had to be far outside Jupiter's orbit.

Kowall followed it for a period of days, working out an approximate orbit, and then started looking for it on photographic plates taken at various observatories months and years earlier, covering the regions where it ought to have been. He located it on some thirty plates, one dating back to 1895, and eventually had enough positions to make it possible to plot an accurate orbit.

From its brightness and distance, it was clear that the new object was a small one, not more than a couple of hundred kilometers in size. Considering its size, it was an asteroid, but its orbit was far outside the asteroid belt at every point, the first asteroid ever discovered with such an orbit.

Kowal named the new asteroid Chiron (KIGH-ron) after the best-known centaur (a creature pictured as having the head and torso of a man fixed onto a horse's body) in the Greek myths.

Chiron has an orbital eccentricity of 0.379. At perihelion it is 1,273,000,000 kilometers (791,000,000 miles) from the sun, or about nine tenths as far from the sun as Saturn is. At aphelion, however, it recedes out to a distance of 2,826,000,000 kilometers (1,756,000,000 miles) from the sun. It is then just about twice as far from the sun as Saturn is.

Chiron is a son of Kronos (Saturn) in the Greek myths and that makes its name all the more appropriate. It is near Saturn's orbit at perihelion but gallops far out, centaur fashion so to speak, in the rest of its orbit.

If its orbit is drawn two-dimensionally as in Figure 19, Chiron seems to cross Saturn's orbit, just as Hidalgo seems to cross Jupiter's orbit. That is an illusion, however, because the actual orbits are slanted to each other. Chiron's orbital inclination is 6.9 degrees as compared to Saturn's 2.5 degrees, so that Chiron's orbit is some hundred million kilometers away from

Fig. 19—Chiron

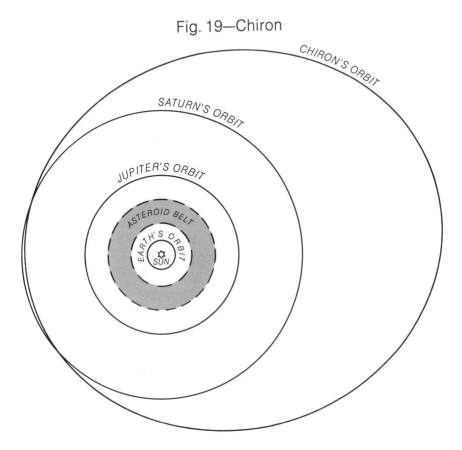

Saturn's orbit (one being above the other) at the points where they seem to cross.

Chiron's period of revolution is 50.6818 years and, as it happens, Chiron was detected when it was only a little past its aphelion and was just about as dim as it ever gets. It was at aphelion in November 1970. It was last at perihelion in August 1945, and will be there again in February 1996. At perihelion, it is about twenty-five times as bright as at aphelion and attains a magnitude of 14.5, but even then it still appears as a star-like point with no trace of any cometary haze—at least not on the photographs in the archives. Close examination in 1996 may yield more information.

It appears to be either a true asteroid that is unusually far out, or a cometoid that is unusually large and that never approaches close enough to develop a haze. Either way, it is a unique object at the moment.

Could there be many asteroids far beyond the asteroid belt? Are there other asteroid belts, or does the asteroid belt we know simply extend outward to the limits of the solar system? Is Chiron merely the largest or closest (or both) of a large group of such objects and will a close search for other small, slow-moving bodies reveal others?

One piece of evidence in favor of Chiron's *not* being unique is that an object similar, in a way, was discovered eighty years ago.

Saturn's outermost satellite, Phoebe, is about the size of Chiron, and because of its peculiar orbit, astronomers have always felt it to be a captured asteroid. Before it was captured it may have followed a Chiron-like orbit about the sun. If so, that would make two, and if there are two there are likely to be many.

# 7

# URANUS

### *The Discovery of Uranus*

In a way, nothing we have yet described totally demolishes the notion of Saturn as a limit to the solar system. One asteroid and numerous comets have orbits that carry them beyond Saturn. In the case of every asteroid and comet we have seen, up to this very moment, at least part of the orbit is, however, located inside the orbit of Saturn.

There may well be cometoids or asteroids that remain beyond the orbit of Saturn at all times, but at least so far we have not seen even one of them.

So far in this book, then, we have not yet described any *visible* body whose orbit lies beyond Saturn at *every* point.

By "visible" we mean something that can be detected by the telescope, or any other instrument, as well as by the unaided eye. This was not always so, of course. Prior to 1600, it was somehow taken for granted that any object in the sky that existed could be seen with the unaided eye; that anything that could not be seen did not exist.

Once the telescope was used, it became apparent at once that there were many objects in the sky that existed and yet were too dim to be seen by the unaided eye. Galileo discovered that everywhere he looked there were numerous stars he couldn't see without the telescope. When he looked at the Milky Way, that band of foggy light turned out to be composed of myriads of very dim stars.

There were even bodies within the solar system that existed and yet could not be seen without the telescope. Galileo discovered the four large satellites of Jupiter almost at once, for instance, while Huygens and Cassini discovered Saturn's rings and five of its satellites.

These new bodies of the solar system, however, were all clearly part of a Jupiter system or a Saturn system. No new *planet* had been discovered and somehow no one expected one to be discovered.

But then came William Herschel, who discovered two of Saturn's satellites in 1789.

Herschel was a self-educated astronomical genius, who built his own telescopes because he could buy none that were good enough, and he ended by building the best that existed in his time. With his telescopes he quickly began to make discoveries. He was the first, for instance, to notice that Mars's axis is tilted in just about the same way that Earth's is.

On March 13, 1781 (eight years before he discovered the Saturnian satellites Mimas and Enceladus), Herschel was busily making careful measurements of the positions of stars. It was his hope that he would finally study every object he could see in the sky.

While he was observing some of the dimmer stars in the constellation Gemini (JEM-ih-nigh, the Twins), he suddenly found himself staring at an object that was not a point of light as the stars were, but showed as a small disc. Herschel increased the magnification of his telescope and the disc looked larger.

Herschel assumed he had discovered a comet, but he had to admit, as he watched it night after night, that it didn't have the appearance of a comet. It wasn't hazy. Instead, the disc showed a sharp boundary. What's more, it moved very slowly, so slowly that it must be well beyond the orbit of Saturn, and no comet had ever been observed so far from the sun.

Once enough observations were made to calculate an orbit, it was clear that that orbit was almost circular, instead of highly elliptical as were those of comets. What's more, the orbit lay far beyond that of Saturn at every point. It was the first body in the solar system that could be seen and that lay beyond the Saturnian boundary of the solar system at *every* point.

Even so, Herschel hesitated to say the unthinkable. Finally, in July 1781 the Russian astronomer Anders Jean Lexell (1740–1784) said it. Herschel, he said, had discovered a new planet, one that was much farther from the sun than Saturn was. It was the first time in recorded history that a new planet had been discovered.

Herschel, as the discoverer, had the right to name the planet. He named it after the British king, George III, and called it "Georgium Sidus," or "George's star."

This name was met with thorough disapproval by astronomers outside Great Britain, who saw no reason why a planet should be named in honor of a British monarch. Some British astronomers suggested the planet be named "Herschel" but that, too, was disapproved of outside Great Britain.

Till that point, all planets had been named after the Greek and Roman gods and goddesses and it was felt that the name of the new planet must cling to that tradition. For one thing that would remove the temptation of having different nations trying to name heavenly objects in accordance with local patriotism.

The German astronomer Johann Elert Bode (BOH-duh, 1747–1826) suggested a logical solution. In Greek mythology Zeus (Jupiter) was the father of Ares (Mars), Aphrodite (Venus), and Hermes (Mercury), so that the planet Jupiter was named for the father of the gods for whom the inner planets (excluding Earth) were named. Moving outward from Jupiter,

Kronos (Saturn) was the father of Zeus (Jupiter) and the grandfather of the gods of the inner planets. Why not continue this progression toward older and older gods as one went away from the sun?

In Greek myths, the father of Kronos (Saturn) was Ouranos, the god of the sky. The Latin spelling of that name was Uranus (YOO-ruh-nus), and why not give that name to the planet?

The suggestion was adopted and the new planet, which Herschel had discovered, has been Uranus ever since.


## The Properties of Uranus

Once Uranus was discovered, it turned out that it was an object that was easily visible in the telescope, and one that could even be seen with the unaided eye (just barely). Why then had it not been discovered long before 1781?

For one thing there was a psychological factor. Astronomers were simply accustomed to the fact that planets were not only visible to the unaided eye, but were very bright objects. In Table 53 the brightness of Uranus is compared with that of Saturn and all the objects in the sky that are brighter than Saturn.

Saturn, the dimmest of the planets known to the ancients, is still the ninth brightest object in the sky. The only brighter objects are the sun, the moon, the four other long-known planets, and the two brightest stars.

Uranus, on the other hand is, only $\frac{1}{244}$ as bright as Saturn, and, much worse, there are some five thousand stars as bright as, or brighter than, Uranus, so that Uranus is lost among them as far as the unaided eye is concerned.

Of course, planets do not have brightness as their only important characteristic. Sirius and Canopus are stars that are of the same order of brightness as the planets and yet they have never been mistaken for planets. That is because the planets

# TABLE 53

## Brightness of Uranus

| OBJECT | MAGNITUDE AT BRIGHTEST | BRIGHTNESS (SATURN = 1) |
|---|---|---|
| Sun | —26.9 | 40,000,000,000 |
| Moon | —12.6 | 76,000 |
| Venus | — 4.3 | 36 |
| Mars | — 2.8 | 13.2 |
| Jupiter | — 2.5 | 10.0 |
| Sirius (star) | — 1.4 | 2.5 |
| Mercury | — 1.2 | 2.1 |
| Canopus (star) | — 0.7 | 1.3 |
| Saturn | — 0.4 | 1.0 |
| **Uranus** | **+ 5.7** | **0.0036** |

move against the background of the stars, while Sirius and Canopus, being stars themselves, do not. If even a dim star moved against the background of the stars, it would be recognized as a planet despite its dimness.

The farther a planet is from the sun, however, the slower its motion across Earth's sky seems (see Table 54). Not only, then, is Uranus only $\frac{1}{244}$ as bright as Saturn in Earth's sky, but it moves only $\frac{1}{3}$ as quickly. It moves slowly enough for that motion to be overlooked, especially in a dim object that does not automatically attract the eye.

One last characteristic of a planet as compared with a star is that a planet shows a disc when it is viewed through a telescope and a star does not. Of course, that is true only if the planet is not too small or not too far away, (see Table 55).

To see Uranus as a disc requires nearly five times the mag-

# TABLE 54

## Apparent Motion of Uranus

| | AVERAGE SHIFT IN EARTH'S SKY | |
|---|---|---|
| PLANET | MINUTES OF ARC PER DAY | DAYS TO MOVE THE WIDTH OF THE MOON |
| Mars | 31.44 | 0.989 |
| Jupiter | 4.99 | 6.23 |
| Saturn | 2.01 | 15.46 |
| **Uranus** | **0.70** | **44.40** |

# TABLE 55

## Apparent Size of Uranus

| PLANET | MAXIMUM APPARENT SIZE (SECONDS OF ARC) | MAGNIFICATION REQUIRED TO PRODUCE A VISIBLE DISC |
|---|---|---|
| Mars | 25.1 | 14.3 |
| Jupiter | 50.0 | 7.2 |
| Saturn | 20.6 | 17.5 |
| **Uranus** | **4.2** | **85.7** |

nification that will do for Saturn and nearly twelve times that which will do for Jupiter.

In appearance, then, Uranus is just a faint star lost among thousands of others. Even with a telescope perfectly capable of showing Saturn as a small disc, Uranus would still look like a star. There would therefore be no reason to return to it after recording its position because there would seem nothing particularly interesting about it. Even if one did return, for some reason, a short time later, it would not have moved enough to do more than make an astronomer think he had made a small mistake in his first calculation of its position.

Uranus could therefore be seen and even recorded a number of times without anyone's suspecting that it was a planet. In 1690 the English astronomer John Flamsteed (1646–1719) observed Uranus, considered it a star, recorded its position, and even gave it a name. He called it "34 Tauri" because at that time it was in the constellation of Taurus the Bull.

In the middle 1700s the French astronomer Pierre Charles Lemonnier (luh-muh-NYAY, 1715–1799) apparently saw and recorded Uranus on thirteen different occasions and was under the impression he had seen thirteen different stars.

Uranus's dimness, which made all these errors possible, was the result, for one thing, of its being at an enormous distance of 2,869,000,000 kilometers (1,783,200,000 miles) from the sun. This is almost exactly twice the distance of Saturn. It takes Uranus 84.0139 years to make one revolution about the sun at that enormous distance, and this is 2.85 times the period of revolution of Saturn.

Both Saturn and Uranus travel in elliptical orbits of low eccentricity, 0.0566 for Saturn and 0.0472 for Uranus. At aphelion Saturn is 1,509,000,000 kilometers (938,000,000 miles) from the sun, and at perihelion Uranus is 2,734,000,000 kilometers (1,699,000,000 miles) from the sun. Even at its closest to the sun, then, Uranus is 1.8 times as far from the sun as Saturn is at its farthest.

With his discovery, then, Herschel had doubled the known diameter of the planetary system.

The recently discovered asteroid Chiron, with its aphelion at 2,826,000,000 kilometers (1,756,000,000 miles) from the sun, reaches a distance just slightly under Uranus's average distance from the sun. Actually Chiron can be farther away from the sun than Uranus is, if Uranus happens to be at its perihelion point while Chiron is at its aphelion. In that case, Chiron can be as much as 92,000,000 kilometers (57,000,000 miles) farther from the sun than Uranus is. However, Chiron's orbit does not carry the asteroid to its aphelion point in that part of Uranus's orbit where the planet's perihelion is. Chiron's orbit and Uranus's orbit do not, therefore, cross. (See Figure 20).

### Fig. 20—The Orbit of Uranus

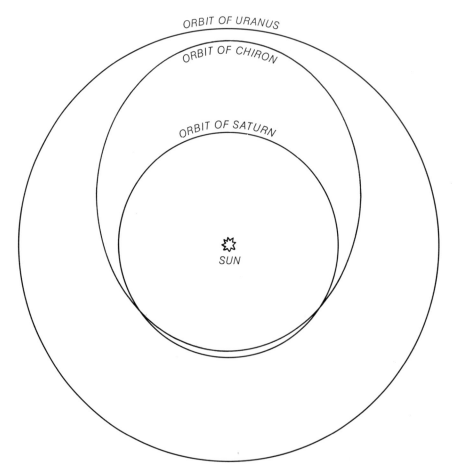

In a two-dimensional diagram, it looks as though Chiron might approach Uranus closely if both were at appropriate parts of their orbits. Thanks to the orbital inclination of Chiron, however, it never approaches more closely than 290,000,000 kilometers (180,000,000 miles) to Uranus.

Of course, Halley's comet moves far beyond even Uranus's orbit and so do uncounted other comets, but no comet has ever been seen that far from the sun. In fact, at the time of Uranus's discovery, no object in the solar system had ever been seen at that distance from the sun.

Once Uranus's distance was known and the width of its disc, as seen in a telescope of known magnification, could be measured, its diameter could be calculated. The best figure we have is 51,800 kilometers (32,200 miles).

Uranus is a giant planet compared to Earth, since it has 4.1 times the radius and 67 times the volume of Earth. Uranus is small compared to Jupiter and Saturn, however. Were Uranus as large as Jupiter, it would have had a magnitude of +3.5, would have been a medium-bright star, and would undoubtedly have been discovered much sooner, perhaps even in ancient times and certainly before the development of the telescope.

Uranus had long been thought to resemble Jupiter and Saturn in its rotational period. That of Uranus had been accepted as 10.82 hours, as compared with Saturn's 10.23 hours and Jupiter's 9.83 hours. A new measurement of Uranus's rotational period in February 1977, however, gave a period of about 25 hours, which is close to that of Mars and Earth.

Favoring the longer period of rotation is the fact that Uranus is much less oblate than either Jupiter or Saturn. Uranus's oblateness is only 0.01, which is twice that of Mars but only a tenth that of Saturn. Uranus's polar diameter is 51,300 kilometers (31,900 miles).

Whether Uranus's period of rotation is Earth-like or Saturn-like is less interesting than the manner in which its axis of rotation is tilted. The tilt is 97.92 degrees, so that the axis lies almost in the plane of revolution about the sun (see Figure 21). Another way of putting it is that Uranus seems to be rolling on its side as it revolves about the sun.

If we imagined ourselves able to stand on Uranus's surface, with an unobstructed view of the heavens, this would create a rather unusual apparent motion for the sun.

If we were standing on Uranus's north pole, for instance, we would see the sun nearly overhead if Uranus were in that part of its orbit where the northern end of its axis of rotation were pointing toward the sun.

Since the axis would not be pointed exactly at the sun (as it would if the axial tip were 90 degrees instead of 97.92 degrees), the sun would appear to be about eight degrees away from the zenith and would circle that zenith once every twenty-five hours.

As Uranus moves in its orbit about the sun, the direction of the axis of rotation would move steadily away from the sun. The sun would thus move about the zenith not in a circle but in a very slowly increasing spiral.

The spiral would widen by four degrees every year, and after

Fig. 21—The Axial Tilt of Uranus

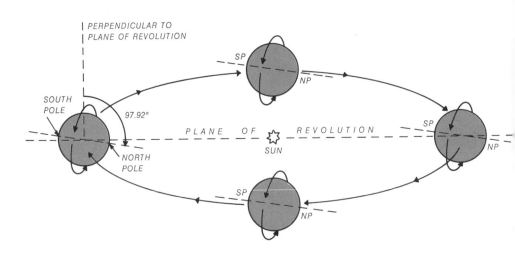

eighteen years it would be skimming the horizon at one end of its circle. For about seven years thereafter, it would sink a small way below the horizon at one end of its circle and rise a small way above it at the other end. Each day it would sink a tiny bit deeper and rise a tiny bit less, until at the end of the seven-year period it would just barely skim the horizon for a few minutes at midday and then it would be gone.

The sun would remain invisible from the north pole for forty years and then would reappear at the other side of the horizon. It would appear for slightly longer intervals each day as it climbed very slowly higher in the sky, until it had lifted itself above the horizon at every point.

It would continue to climb higher until it made a small circle 16 degrees in diameter about the zenith, after which it would begin to sink again and the whole cycle would start all over. The entire cycle would take eighty-four years.

From a spot on Uranus's equator, the sun would seem to spiral slowly from the northern horizon to the southern horizon and back again in eighty-four years.

As seen from Uranus, the sun has an apparent width of only 1.6 minutes of arc. It would take twenty objects the size of the sun as seen from Uranus, placed side by side and touching, to stretch across the apparent diameter of the sun as seen from Earth.

The sun as seen from Uranus would be only a point of light, rather like Venus as seen from Earth—but much brighter, of course.

At Uranus's vast distance from the sun, the light and heat reaching Uranus is only $\frac{1}{368}$ that which reaches Earth. Even so, the sun's shrunken dot remains about 1,250 times as bright as the full moon does to us on Earth. Its magnitude would be —20.5 and it would be 40,000,000 times as bright as Sirius, the brightest star.

Someone who knew nothing about astronomy, observing the

sky from Uranus with the unaided eye, would be sure to notice that the sun is widely different from all the rest of the stars.

The distant sun is not very efficient in warming Uranus, which has an average surface temperature of —216° C. (—356° F.) or only 57° above absolute zero. Nevertheless, when one of Uranus's poles faces the sun in the course of Uranus's revolution, its hemisphere is about 20 percent warmer than the other.

Because of the peculiar way in which Uranus rotates, the poles receive more sunlight in the course of the Uranian year than the equator does. The poles are therefore the warmest part of Uranus; though perhaps the proper way of saying it is that the poles are the least incredibly frigid.

### The Satellites of Uranus

There are no bright planets in Uranus's sky. Saturn is its nearest neighbor and when it is at its brightest in Uranus's sky, its magnitude is only 4.5 so that it would appear to be a fairly dim star.

Nevertheless there are, in addition to the sun, five objects brighter than Saturn and more noticeable than any of the stars in Uranus's sky, for Uranus has satellites.

Once Herschel had discovered Uranus he kept his eye on it, and in 1787 he noted two satellites circling it. Eventually the inner one was named Titania (tih-TAY-nee-uh) and the outer one Oberon (OH-buh-ron).

These were the first worlds of the solar system with names that were not taken from the Greek and Roman myths. Titania and Oberon were the queen and king of the fairies in Shakespeare's *A Midsummer Night's Dream.*

Shakespeare did not make them up, however. Titania is used by the Roman poet Ovid as an alternate name for Diana, the goddess of the moon. Oberon is a French version of Alberich, who was the king of the elves in medieval German and Scandi- navian legends, and who appears under that name as a de- formed and malicious gnome in Wagner's operas concerning the Ring of the Nibelungen.

In 1851 the English astronomer William Lassell (1799– 1880) discovered two more satellites, closer to Uranus than either of Herschel's. These were named Ariel (AIR-ee-el) and Umbriel (UM-bree-el).

Ariel continues the Shakespeare touch, for that represents another fairy from his plays; this time, a spirit of the air, in *The Tempest*. Umbriel is a spirit as well, but is non-Shakes- pearian. It is to be found in the mock-epic *The Rape of the Lock* by Alexander Pope, where it is a gloomy, sighing spirit. Pope invented the name from the Latin *umbra*, meaning "shadow."

Finally, in 1948, Kuiper (who discovered Titan's atmosphere) detected a fifth satellite, closer to Uranus than any of the others, and called it Miranda (mih-RAN-duh). This is the only one of the five satellites not named for a spirit, but it carries on the Shakespearian tradition, since Miranda is the heroine of *The Tempest*.

The order of the discovery of these satellites is, not surpris- ingly, in the order of their brightness. Titania and Oberon, the first pair to be discovered, are of the fourteenth magnitude at their brightest. Ariel and Umbriel, the second pair, are of the fifteenth magnitude. Miranda is of the seventeenth magnitude.

The Uranian satellites all revolve in nearly perfect circles about Uranus, and move exactly in the plane of the planet's equator. This means that the plane of the revolution of the satellites is more or less perpendicular to the plane of Uranus's revolution about the sun. It was this queer up-and-down motion of the satellites that first gave astronomers the hint that Uranus's axis was tipped to so large an extent.

The satellite system of Uranus is a rather compact one (see Table 56 and Figure 22). Even Oberon, the farthest of the

# TABLE 56

## Period of Revolution and Distance of the Satellites of Uranus

| | | DISTANCE FROM URANUS | | |
| | PERIOD OF REVOLUTION | | | URANUS'S |
| SATELLITE | (DAYS) | KILOMETERS | MILES | RADIUS = 1 |
| --- | --- | --- | --- | --- |
| Miranda | 1.414 | 130,000 | 80,800 | 5.02 |
| Ariel | 2.520 | 192,000 | 119,000 | 7.41 |
| Umbriel | 4.144 | 267,000 | 166,000 | 10.3 |
| Titania | 8.706 | 438,000 | 272,000 | 16.9 |
| Oberon | 13.463 | 586,000 | 364,000 | 22.6 |

Uranian satellites, is closer to Uranus than Europa is to Jupiter, and is almost as close as Rhea is to Saturn. If Uranus has distant satellites which are captured asteroids, as is true for Jupiter and Saturn, they are too small to see at Uranus's distance— at least so far.

From the distance and period of revolution of any satellite, the mass of the planet it circles can be estimated. The mass of Uranus is thus known to be 14.54 times that of the Earth. That, however, is not quite $\frac{1}{6}$ the mass of Saturn and not quite $\frac{1}{20}$ that of Jupiter.

From its volume and mass, the density of Uranus turns out to be 1.21 times the density of water. That is considerably higher than the density of Saturn and very nearly the density of Jupiter.

This does not mean, however, that Uranus necessarily has the same structure as Jupiter. Jupiter is a far larger and more massive planet and its intense gravitational field compresses it far more than Uranus can be compressed. For Uranus to at-

Fig. 22—The Satellites of Uranus

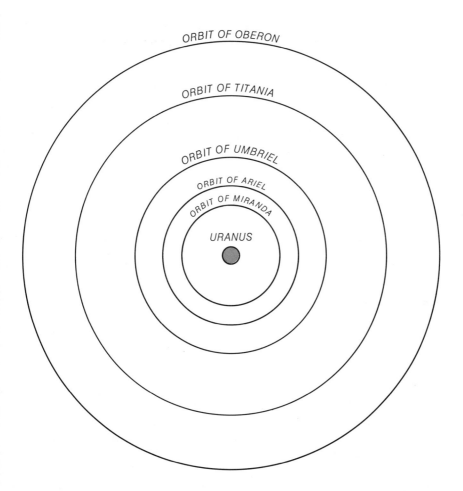

tain the same density as Jupiter with so much less compression, it follows that Uranus must contain a smaller percentage of hydrogen and helium than Jupiter and Saturn do and a larger percentage of the more massive molecules that make up the ices.

From the composition of Uranus, we might picture it as made of cometary matter which is mostly icy—as a gigantic cometoid, just as Earth and the other inner planets are gigantic asteroids. Jupiter and Saturn are neither, of course, but are made up of materials like those which make up the sun; they are tiny stars that are just not large enough to break into nuclear flame.

From the spectrum of the light reflected by Uranus, in 1932 Rupert Wildt suggested the presence of methane in its atmosphere. Uranus shows up as a greenish-blue in color, probably because its atmosphere contains large quantities of methane.

The best figures available on the size and mass of the satellites of Uranus are quite uncertain, but for what they are worth, they are given in Table 57.

# TABLE 57

## Diameter and Mass of the Satellites of Uranus

| | DIAMETER | | |
| SATELLITE | KILOMETERS | MILES | (MOON = 1) MASS |
| --- | --- | --- | --- |
| Miranda | 240 | 150 | 0.001 |
| Ariel | 700 | 430 | 0.018 |
| Umbriel | 500 | 310 | 0.007 |
| Titania | 1,000 | 620 | 0.059 |
| Oberon | 900 | 560 | 0.034 |

Unlike Jupiter and Saturn (and Earth), Uranus does not have any large satellites. Even the largest, Titania, is of moderate size only. The total mass of the five satellites of Uranus is only ⅛ that of our moon.

The apparent diameter of the five satellites of Uranus as seen from the Uranian "surface" is given in Table 58. Of the

# TABLE 58

## Apparent Diameter of Satellites of Uranus as Seen in Uranus's Sky

| SATELLITE | APPARENT DIAMETER (MINUTES OF ARC) |
|-----------|-----------|
| Miranda | 6.2 |
| Ariel | 12.8 |
| Umbriel | 6.2 |
| Titania | 7.6 |
| Oberon | 7.1 |

five satellites, four would be just barely made out as tiny orbs. Only Ariel would show a distinct disc, being one third as large in apparent diameter as our moon seems to us. They would, however, be lit by the far distant sun, even though very dimly, and if we could imagine Uranian astronomers watching the sky, the five satellites would attract attention not so much by their size or brightness as by their rapid motion across the sky against the pattern of the fixed stars.

The sky as viewed from any of the satellites would, of course, contain Uranus. This would be true, at least, if the sky were viewed from the proper hemisphere, for it is very likely that each satellite, as it revolves about Uranus, keeps one face always to the planet.

From any of the satellites, green-tinted Uranus would seem enormous compared to the size of the moon as seen from Earth (see Table 59). Lit by the light of the distant, dim sun, how-

# TABLE 59

## Size of Uranus as Seen from Its Satellites

| SATELLITE | DIAMETER OF URANUS (DEGREES) | AREA OF URANUS (MOON = 1) | BRIGHTNESS OF URANUS (MOON = 1) |
|---|---|---|---|
| Miranda | 22.5 | 1,870 | 30.5 |
| Ariel | 15.4 | 890 | 14.5 |
| Umbriel | 11.1 | 460 | 7.4 |
| Titania | 6.8 | 170 | 2.8 |
| Oberon | 5.1 | 100 | 1.6 |

ever, Uranus would be only softly luminous and would not deliver as much light as we would expect from its apparent size.

The phases of Uranus would be complicated indeed as seen from the satellites.

For a long period, at the time when one of the poles of Uranus was pointed in the direction of the sun, Uranus would be in the half-phase. That and the position of the sun would seem unchanging.

Actually, Uranus would not be exactly in the half-phase, and as the satellite went around Uranus it would see it slighty more than half-lit on one side and slightly less than half-lit on the other. The phase boundary would oscillate back and forth with a period equal to that of the satellite's revolution.

The oscillation increases slowly, and after twenty years the sun has moved to the point where it is eclipsed by Uranus each revolution. By then Uranus approaches the full cycle of phases with each of the satellite's revolutions.

As the sun begins to move out from beyond Uranus in the other direction, the oscillation of the phase boundary begins to decrease again, so that after another twenty years or so Uranus settles down to the nearly half-phase again, but is now lighted from the other direction.

The change then begins to move in the opposite direction, until it is restored as it was originally, the entire cycle taking eighty-four years. From Uranus the one satellite that is large enough to show more or less clear phases, Ariel, follows a similar pattern in miniature.

### The Rings of Uranus

In 1973 a British astronomer, Gordon Taylor, calculated that Uranus would move in front of a ninth-magnitude star, SAO 158687. It wasn't often that a planet moved in front of a bright star, even one only as bright as the ninth magnitude (far too dim to see with the unaided eye), and it was exciting news.

Astronomers made preparations at once to observe this "occultation" which was slated to take place four years later, on March 10, 1977. As Uranus approached the star and passed in front of it, the starlight would pass through the upper reaches of Uranus's atmosphere. At first the starlight would pass through a region of such thin gas that it would scarcely be affected. As Uranus moved in, however, the starlight would pass through thicker and thicker regions of the atmosphere and grow dimmer and dimmer until the star was altogether hidden. As Uranus passed by, the star would appear and grow brighter and brighter until it was restored to its full brightness.

The manner in which the starlight gradually dimmed on one

side of Uranus and gradually brightened on the other side might well tell astronomers something about the temperature, pressure, and composition of Uranus's atmosphere.

On March 10, 1977, James L. Elliot of Cornell University and several associates were in an airplane that carried them high above the distorting and obscuring effects of the lower atmosphere. From that airplane they prepared to observe the occultation.

Before Uranus reached the star, the starlight suddenly dimmed for about seven seconds and then brightened again. The intensity of the light was being measured by a delicate instrument and there could be no mistake.

Apparently something that wasn't visible to the eye had gotten in front of the star and had momentarily blocked the light. It might be a small satellite, one that was too small to see and that was closer to Uranus than Miranda was. If that were so, it was quite a coincidence that the satellite should have happened to move in its orbit in such a way as to get exactly in between the star and Earth.

But then, as Uranus continued to approach the star still more closely, there were four more brief episodes of dimming, for a second each. Four more satellites, smaller still, each one of which just managed to get in the way of the starlight? A coincidence like that was unbelievable.

Uranus eventually passed in front of the star, and as the planet moved away on the other side there was the same dimming of starlight in reverse: four times for a second each and then a fifth time for seven seconds. (Other astronomers studying Uranus at the same time also noticed the dimming effects.)

The only way of explaining what had happened was to suppose not satellites, but rings. Uranus had rings as Saturn did, and nobody had ever seen them before. There seemed to be five rings around Uranus, in fact, but closer observation of another, even fainter star, in front of which Uranus moved on April 10,

1978, revealed a total of nine rings. The innermost one is 42,000 kilometers (25,200 miles) from the center of Uranus, and the outermost one is 50,800 kilometers (30,500 miles) from the center of Uranus.

In terms of Uranus's radius, the ring system stretched from 1.62 to 1.96 times the radius and was well within the Roche limit, as was to be expected (see Figure 23).

Fig. 23—The Rings of Uranus

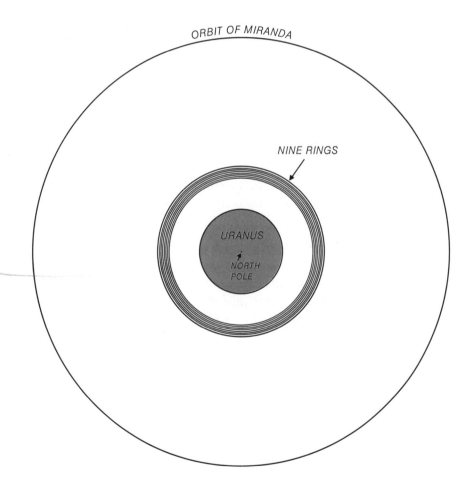

Why had it taken so long to discover the rings of Uranus?

First, Uranus is distant. The total distance light must travel from the sun to Uranus and back to Earth is four times as great as the distance it must travel from the sun to Saturn and back to Earth. All things being equal, the Uranian ring-system would be only $\frac{1}{16}$ as bright as the Saturnian ring-system.

Second, all things are not equal. The Uranian rings are very narrow. The thin ones that obscured the star for only a second apiece are each about 12 kilometers (7.5 miles) wide or less, and the wide one that obscured it for 7 seconds might be 85 kilometers (50 miles) wide. The total width of the Uranian rings is about 170 kilometers (105 miles) as compared with a total width of 57,000 kilometers (35,000 miles) for the Saturnian rings.

Third, the material in the Uranian rings is more thinly strewn than that within the Saturnian rings. In passing behind the Uranian rings, the star was not blanked out altogether, but was merely dimmed.

Fourth, the Uranian rings are not of the same composition as the Saturnian rings. The Saturnian rings reflect more than half the light that falls on them and are probably composed of icy particles. The Uranian rings reflect less than a twentieth of the light that falls upon them and must be particles of dark rock.

Lumping all these differences—distance, width, density, and albedo—we might estimate that the total light reaching us from the Uranian rings is only about $\frac{1}{3,000,000}$ the light that reaches us from the Saturnian rings.

No wonder it took astronomers so long to spot the Uranian rings. But for the lucky happening of Uranus moving in front of a not-too-dim star, we might still have no idea of their existence.

# 8

## NEPTUNE

### *The Discovery of Neptune*

For years after Uranus was discovered, astronomers followed its position in the sky with great interest. If it were only a matter of Uranus and the sun, Uranus would move in a perfect ellipse which could be easily calculated. However, both Saturn and Jupiter exerted tiny pulls upon it. When either planet was behind Uranus in its trip about the sun, the pull was exerted backward, and tended to slow Uranus's motion. When either planet moved ahead of Uranus, the pull was exerted forward, and tended to speed it up.

As Saturn and Jupiter each moved in its own orbit, the pattern of pulls on Uranus changed steadily, and the calculation of Uranus's changing position was therefore rather complicated.

In 1821, the French astronomer Alexis Bouvard (boo-VAHR, 1767–1843) calculated Uranus's orbit very carefully. He took all the observations that had been made since the planet's discovery and added those observations he could find that were made before the discovery, when various astronomers thought they were determining the position of a star. He then recalculated the gravitational influences of Jupiter and Saturn on Uranus.

When he was all through, he found the orbit he had worked out didn't represent Uranus's actual motion. Uranus's actual motion was such that at times Uranus was as much as 2 minutes of arc away from its calculated position. This discrepancy in its position amounted to only $\frac{1}{15}$ the apparent diameter of the moon, but it was enough to upset astronomers. Their calculations should be much better than that.

The easiest way of accounting for this discrepancy in position was to suppose that there was some additional pull on Uranus, besides that of Jupiter and Saturn.

There was, of course, the pull of the other planets: Mars, Earth, Venus, and Mercury. But those planets were too small and too far away to be of any account. To explain Uranus's wandering away from its proper position, there had to be a large planet doing the pulling. And if there were such a planet closer to the sun than Uranus, it would have been seen long before—undoubtedly even before Uranus was discovered.

It followed that there had to be a planet beyond Uranus that was sometimes speeding it up and sometimes slowing it down, a planet that had not yet been discovered and whose pull had therefore not been taken into account.

Well, then, could one just look for the planet and find it?

That was far more easily said than done. Uranus was just barely visible to the unaided eye, and was so far away that it took a good telescope to show it as a disc and careful study from day to day to pick up its slow drift against the stars. A still more distant planet, unless it were an unexectedly huge giant, would be dimmer still, quite invisible to the unaided eye, with a still smaller disc, and an even slower rate of motion across the sky. All the signs of planethood would be faint indeed.

What is more, the dimmer the planet, the more stars there are that are as bright. A dim planet has to be picked out from among the stars that crowd about it, and the dimmer the planet, the greater the crowds of stars that are produced by the magnification of the telescope designed to make out the planet.

Clearly, the discovery of a planet more distant than Uranus was going to be a very difficult job. Astronomers could comb the skies for years without finding it, and few were willing to undertake such an arduous job when they might end up finding nothing.

Perhaps, though, there might be some way of knowing in advance where the planet might be. There was some indication that this might be possible.

In 1766 a German astronomer, Johann Daniel Titius (TIH-tee-oos, 1729–1796) had pointed out an interesting mathematical relationship in the distances of the planets. Suppose, for instance, we begin by writing a series of numbers that start with 0 and 3 and thereafter double each number to get the one after, thus: 0, 3, 6, 12, 24, 48, 96, 192, 384 . . .

Next, suppose we add 4 to each number: 4, 7, 10, 16, 28, 52, 100, 196, 388 . . . Finally, suppose we list the average distances of the planets from the sun, counting Earth's distance from the sun as 10. If we compare the two series of numbers, the results are as given in Table 60.

Titius's numbers provoked little interest, but in 1772 Bode (who was later to give Uranus its name) publicized them. Thereafter it was called "Bode's law," but in recent years it has more properly been called "the Titius-Bode law."

Astronomers found the Titius numbers interesting but useless—until Uranus was discovered in 1781. The distance of Uranus from the sun, on an Earth = 10 basis, turned out to be 191.82, very close to the Titius number 196. That suddenly gave the numbers importance; they seemed to represent a map of the solar system.

Interest was at once riveted on the Titius number 28, which was not represented by any planet. Astronomers began to talk about the "gap" between Mars and Jupiter, and to make plans

# TABLE 60

## The Titius-Bode Law

| PLANET | DISTANCE FROM SUN (EARTH = 10) | TITIUS NUMBERS |
|--------|--------------------------------|----------------|
| Mercury | 3.87 | 4 |
| Venus | 7.23 | 7 |
| Earth | 10.00 | 10 |
| Mars | 15.23 | 16 |
| | | 28 |
| Jupiter | 52.03 | 52 |
| Saturn | 95.39 | 100 |
| | | 196 |
| | | 388 |

to search the sky for a planet at a distance equivalent to Titius number 28. Ceres was discovered just before the search began in a quite accidental manner (see page 140) but the search continued and produced three more asteroids.

The distance of Ceres from the sun proved to be 27.7 on an Earth = 10 basis, very close to the 28. To be sure, other asteroids were discovered, but 28 turned out to represent, quite closely, the average distance of the asteroids from the sun.

By the time Bouvard pointed out the discrepancy in Uranus's orbital motion, astronomers took it for granted that if there was a planet beyond Uranus, its distance from the sun would have to be at or near Titius number 388. That would make it twice as far from the sun as Uranus is.

Suppose, then, there were a planet at such a distance, and suppose it to be about the size of Uranus and to move in a circular orbit about the sun in the same plane as Uranus's orbit. It would have to exert a particular gravitational pull on Uranus which could be calculated.

But suppose there were a gravitational pull on Uranus that accounted for its position's not agreeing with theory. Given that pull, perhaps one could work backward and determine the orbit of the unknown planet and its position at the moment of calculation.

In 1841 a twenty-two-year-old mathematics student at Cambridge University in England tackled the problem and worked at it in his spare time. His name was John Couch Adams (1819–1892) and by September 1845 he had finished. The unknown planet, he decided, had to be in a certain spot in the constellation Aquarius as of October 1, 1845.

Naturally, it was too much to expect that it would be in exactly the calculated spot. The actual planet might be a little larger than Uranus or a little smaller, a little more distant than Titius number 388 or a little less distant, possessing an orbit a little more eccentric or with a little more inclination to the ecliptic than expected. All these things would mean it would have to be in a slightly different position—but perhaps not very far away. Some astronomer with a telescope would have to search some distance to every side of the calculated position. It would be tedious but not nearly as bad as searching for the planet with no hint at all.

Adams gave the result of his calculations to James Challis (1803–1882), the director of the Cambridge Observatory. Adams hoped that Challis would search the appropriate part of the sky, but Challis felt he had better things to do, and passed the buck by giving Adams a letter of recommendation to the Astronomer Royal, George Biddell Airy (1801–1892).

Twice Adams visited Airy's home only to find him away. A third time, Airy was at dinner and refused to be disturbed. Adams left his calculations and when Airy leafed through them he wasn't impressed, so the matter was left to die.

Meanwhile a young French astronomer, Urbain Jean Joseph Leverrier (le-ver-YAY, 1811–1877) was also working on the problem, quite independently. He completed his work about half a year after Adam and got just about the same answer. He also sent his calculations to Airy.

Airy, having received the same material twice from two different men, was finally impressed. He therefore wrote to Challis at Cambridge in July 1846, asking him to study the sky in the neighborhood of the indicated position to see if he could find a planet.

Challis was still reluctant to do the work, which he thought would come to nothing. It was three weeks after he got Airy's request before he even started and then he proceeded very slowly indeed. So uninterested was he that he failed to check stars observed on one day with the same stars observed on another day in order to see whether any of them had moved relative to the rest—which would be a sure sign it was a planet.

On September 18, meanwhile, Leverrier, having heard nothing from Cambridge, decided to try elsewhere. He wrote to the Berlin Observatory and its director, Encke (of Encke's Comet), asked one of his astronomers, Johann Gottfried Galle (GAHL-uh, 1812–1910), to do the checking.

Galle had a lucky break. The Berlin Observatory had been preparing a careful series of star charts and Galle had a very good one, prepared just half a year before, of just the region of the sky in which the new planet might be. That meant he didn't have to observe all the stars from day to day to see if any of them had moved. All he had to do was observe the stars and compare each with its position on the chart. Any star that was out of position was very likely to be the missing planet.

On the night of September 23, 1846, Galle got to work with his assistant, Heinrich Ludwig d'Arrest (dah-REH, 1822–1875). Galle was at the telescope, moving methodically over the field, calling out the positions of stars one by one, while D'Arrest was at the chart, checking those positions. They had been working for barely an hour when Galle called off the position of an eighth-magnitude star and D'Arrest said, in excitement, "That's not on the chart."

It was the planet! It was less than a degree from the calculated spot.

Once the news was announced, Challis hurriedly went over his own observations and found that he had seen Neptune on four different occasions but had never compared positions and so had not known what he had.

There was some dispute over who deserved the credit for the discovery, but nowadays it is generally felt that Adams and Leverrier share the credit equally.

It turned out, as it happened, that the planet had been observed long before it was realized to be the planet beyond Uranus. On May 8, 1795, only fourteen years after the discovery of Uranus, the French astronomer Joseph Jérôme de Lalande (lah-LAHND, 1732–1807) noted a star whose position he recorded. Two days later he observed it again and was mortified to note that he had made a mistake in the position. He recorded the new position and forgot the matter. Actually he had made no mistake. The "star" had moved in those two days, because Lalande, without knowing it, had been looking at the planet beyond Uranus.

What was the new planet to be named? Some French astronomers suggested it be named "Leverrier" after the discoverer, but non-French astronomers unanimously objected.

Leverrier himself, noting that the new planet was even greener in color than Uranus, suggested calling it Neptune (NEP-tyoon) for the Roman god of the green sea (equivalent to the Greek god Poseidon). The suggestion was adopted and Neptune it was.

## The Outer Planets

When Neptune's orbit was worked out, it turned out to be nearly circular with an eccentricity of 0.0086, a figure that is lower than that of any planet but Venus. The orbital inclination of Neptune is 1.77° compared to Uranus's 0.77°. In both respects, Neptune's orbit was close to what Adams and Leverrier had assumed it would be in order to simplify their calculations, and that had helped them get an answer that was close to the facts.

In one respect, however, Neptune was a shattering surprise. It destroyed the Titius-Bode law. Neptune was at an enormous distance from the sun, to be sure—a distance of 4,496,600,000 kilometers (2,794,100,000 miles). This placed it one and a half times as far from the sun as Uranus was, but it wasn't enough. If there were really something to the Titius-Bode law, Neptune should have been about 5,800,000,000 kilometers (3,600,000,-000 miles) from the sun (see Table 61 and Figure 24).

Because of its great distance from the sun, Neptune moved in its orbit at a speed that was less than that of any of the

# TABLE 61

## Distance of the Outer Planets

| | DISTANCE | | | |
| PLANET | KILOMETERS | MILES | EARTH = 10 | TITIUS NUMBER |
| --- | --- | --- | --- | --- |
| Jupiter | 778,300,000 | 483,600,000 | 52.03 | 52 |
| Saturn | 1,427,000,000 | 886,700,000 | 95.39 | 100 |
| Uranus | 2,869,600,000 | 1,783,200,000 | 191.82 | 196 |
| Neptune | 4,496,600,000 | 2,794,200,000 | 300.58 | 388 |

Fig. 24—The Orbit of Neptune

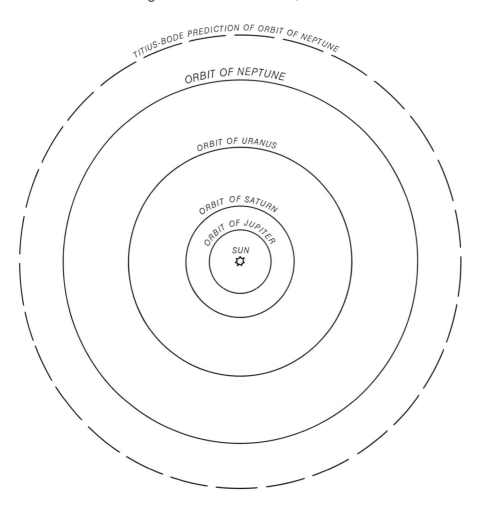

longer-known planets and took a longer time to revolve about the sun (see Table 62). In all the time since Neptune has been discovered, it has not yet had time to complete one turn about its orbit. It will not be till 2010 that it will return to the spot in Aquarius in which it was discovered.

## TABLE 62

### Orbits of the Outer Planets

| | | ORBITAL SPEED | |
| PLANET | PERIOD OF REVOLUTION (YEARS) | KILOMETERS PER SECOND | MILES PER SECOND |
|---|---|---|---|
| Jupiter | 11.862 | 13.1 | 8.1 |
| Saturn | 29.458 | 9.6 | 6.0 |
| Uranus | 84.014 | 6.8 | 4.2 |
| Neptune | 164.793 | 5.4 | 3.4 |

Neptune's great distance accounts for the difficulty of its discovery in several ways. Whereas Uranus has, at its brightest, a magnitude of 5.52, Neptune's is never more than 7.84. Neptune is therefore only about ⅑ as bright as Uranus and is never visible to the unaided eye.

Neptune's apparent motion moves it across the sky only 21.5 seconds of arc on the average. This is only half the apparent motion of Uranus. It would take 86.5 days for Neptune to move a distance equal to the diameter of the moon, as compared with 42.9 days for Uranus to do so.

Finally, Neptune's apparent diameter is at most 2.4 seconds of arc as compared with 4.2 seconds of arc for Uranus. At equal magnifications, Neptune appears only three fifths the diameter and only one third the area of Uranus.

Considering Neptune's greater dimness, slower motion, and smaller orb, there would have been little chance of its being discovered accidentally as Uranus was. The Adams-Leverrier calculations were a pretty strong necessity.

From the apparent size of Neptune and from its distance, its diameter could be determined and it turned out to be roughly of the size of Uranus (see Table 63). It made the fourth planet

# TABLE 63

## Diameters of the Outer Planets

| | DIAMETERS | | |
| PLANETS | KILOMETERS | MILES | EARTH = 1 |
| --- | --- | --- | --- |
| Jupiter | 143,200 | 89,000 | 11.23 |
| Saturn | 120,000 | 74,600 | 9.41 |
| Uranus | 51,800 | 32,200 | 4.06 |
| Neptune | 49,500 | 30,800 | 3.88 |

to prove to be larger than the Earth. To this day the four outer planets, Jupiter, Saturn, Uranus, and Neptune, remain the only bodies in the solar system (other than the sun itself) to be larger than the Earth (see Figure 25). They are sometimes referred to as the four giant planets, for that reason.

The rotation period of Neptune is as hard to determine as is the case of Uranus. The most recent measurements, taken in early 1977, make it appear that Neptune, like Uranus, rotates more slowly than had been thought (see Table 64).

Although Neptune is very like Uranus in size, color, and period of rotation, there is one difference we might mention here. Neptune's axis of rotation is tipped from the perpendicular to the plane of revolution by 28.8°. This is just slightly more

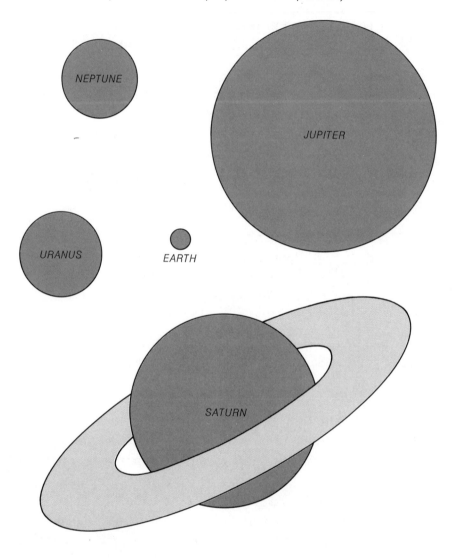

Fig. 25—Relative Size of the Outer Planets
*(Earth shown for purpose of comparison)*

# TABLE 64

## Rotation of the Outer Planets

| PLANET | PERIOD OF ROTATION | | EQUATORIAL SPEED OF ROTATION | | OBLATENESS |
| | HOURS | DAYS | KILOMETERS PER SECOND | MILES PER SECOND | |
|---|---|---|---|---|---|
| Jupiter | 9.83 | 0.41 | 12.71 | 7.90 | 0.064 |
| Saturn | 10.23 | 0.43 | 10.24 | 6.36 | 0.102 |
| Uranus | 25 | 1.05 | 1.81 | 1.12 | 0.010 |
| Neptune | 22 | 0.92 | 1.96 | 1.22 | 0.024 |

than the tipping of the axes of Earth, Mars, and Saturn. Unlike Uranus, Neptune does not roll on its side as it moves around the sun.

### *Triton*
Neptune is even more isolated than Uranus. From Neptune, the sun has an apparent diameter of only 1 minute of arc, but that starlike point still shines with a light equal to 515 times that of the full moon as seen from Earth. The feeble heat from the distant sun keeps Neptune's "surface" at a temperature of —228° C. (—378° F.), or only 45 degrees C. above absolute zero.

From Neptune, Jupiter is never seen farther than 10 degrees from the sun, Saturn never farther than 18.5 degrees, and Uranus never farther than 32.5 degrees. All three are barely on the border of unaided-eye visibility. In general you can say that if the human eye were on the upper level of the cloud layer of Neptune, all it would see would be the fixed stars, the much brighter pinpoint of the sun—and one more thing.

On October 10, 1846, less than three weeks after Neptune was first sighted, a satellite for it was discovered by the English astronomer William Lassell.

The satellite was named Triton (TRY-ton), who was a son of Poseidon (Neptune) in the Greek myths. In a way, this is a poor name. We now have a situation in which the first and largest Saturnian satellite to be discovered is Titan, the first and largest Uranian satellite is Titania, the first and largest Neptunian satellite is Triton. The chances for confusion are all too obvious.

The most interesting thing about Triton is its magnitude. Its magnitude is, at its brightest, 13.6. This is very dim, of course, but Triton is brighter than either of the two Uranian satellites then known, Titania and Oberon, which have magnitudes of 13.9 and 14.1 respectively. Considering that Triton was one and a half times as far from Earth as Titania and Oberon were, and that Triton was illuminated in a sunlight less than half as intense as that which struck Titania and Oberon, it was clear that Triton had to be rather large.

And so it was. The diameter of Triton is 3800 kilometers (2400 miles), which is 1.1 times the diameter of the moon. Triton is larger than the two smaller Galilean satellites of Jupiter, but it is smaller than Titan, Ganymede, and Callisto.

It was the first large satellite to be discovered since Titan, nearly two hundred years before, and was the seventh altogether. It is better than average in mass among these large ones (see Table 65). The seven large satellites have a total mass just ten times that of the moon or two times that of Mercury.

Triton circles Neptune in an orbit that is almost a perfect circle, and its distance from Neptune's center is 355,000 kilometers (221,000 miles). It is just a trifle closer to Neptune than the moon is to the Earth.

Despite the fact that Triton has about the same length of orbit to travel that the moon does, Triton completes its turn

# TABLE 65

## Masses of the Large Satellites

| SATELLITE | MASS (MOON = 1) |
|-----------|-----------------|
| Ganymede | 2.027 |
| Titan | 1.905 |
| Triton | 1.8 |
| Callisto | 1.448 |
| Io | 1.213 |
| Moon | 1.000 |
| Europa | 0.663 |

in 5.87654 days, or in about one fifth the time the moon takes. This is an immediate indication that Neptune is considerably more massive than the Earth. In fact, Neptune's mass is considerably greater than that of Uranus (see Table 66) despite Neptune's smaller size.

This discrepancy shows up in more marked fashion when the density of the outer planets is considered (see Table 67).

# TABLE 66

## Masses of the Outer Planets

| PLANET | MASS (EARTH = 1) |
|--------|------------------|
| Jupiter | 317.9 |
| Saturn | 95.1 |
| Uranus | 14.5 |
| Neptune | 17.2 |

# TABLE 67

## Densities of the Outer Planets

| | DENSITY | |
| PLANET | EARTH = 1 | WATER = 1 |
| --- | --- | --- |
| Jupiter | 0.238 | 1.31 |
| Saturn | 0.128 | 0.71 |
| Uranus | 0.219 | 1.21 |
| Neptune | 0.303 | 1.67 |

Neptune, although the smallest of the four outer planets, is the densest. Although it is gaseous in its outer regions, and undoubtedly consists largely of ices as Uranus does, Neptune must have a rocky core larger in comparison to its total volume than is true for the other outer planets.

The unusual density of Neptune is also reflected in its surface gravity (see Table 68).

# TABLE 68

## Gravitational Pull of the Outer Planets

| | | ESCAPE VELOCITY | |
| PLANET | SURFACE GRAVITY (EARTH = 1) | KILOMETERS PER SECOND | MILES PER SECOND |
| --- | --- | --- | --- |
| Jupiter | 2.34 | 59.5 | 37.0 |
| Saturn | 0.93 | 35.6 | 21.8 |
| Uranus | 0.79 | 21.2 | 13.1 |
| Neptune | 1.12 | 23.6 | 14.7 |

The more massive a planet, the greater the intensity of its gravitation. If, however, it is a large planet, its surface is far away from its center and that decreases the pull of gravity at the surface. If the planet is particularly low in density, the surface is particularly far outward for its mass, and the surface gravity is surprisingly low.

That is why Saturn, with its extraordinarily low density, manages to have a surface gravity just under that of the Earth, for all the fact that it has a much greater mass than Earth. Uranus, though one of the large planets, has a surface gravity that is only four fifths that of Earth.

Neptune, however, is dense enough to have a surface gravity greater than that of Earth. Indeed, of all the bodies in the solar system, only the sun, Jupiter, and Neptune have surface gravities larger than that of Earth.

The escape velocity is somewhat better as an indication of total mass. All the large outer planets have escape velocities that are greater than that of Earth (which is 11.2 kilometers per second, or 7.0 miles per second). Even Uranus, the least massive of the outer planets, has an escape velocity nearly twice that of Earth.

Incidentally, if we consider the mass of the outer planets, the mass of Jupiter is 2.5 times as great as that of the other three outer planets combined. All four planets together make up 99 percent of all the matter in the solar system outside the sun itself. The other planets (including the Earth), satellites, asteroids, and comets all together make up the remaining 1 percent. It might almost be said of the solar system that it consists of one star, two large planets, two medium-sized planets, and debris.

The large satellites of Jupiter and Saturn all revolve in the plane of the equator of their planet. Triton, like our moon, does not do so. Triton's orbit seems to be tipped by 20 degrees to the plane of Neptune's equator.

Triton, however, follows its orbit in the retrograde direction, moving in the direction opposite to that in which Neptune is rotating. Astronomers therefore prefer to consider Triton's orbit as being tipped by 160 degrees to the plane of Neptune's equator (see Figure 26). Why this should be is rather a mystery.

If we could imagine ourselves standing on Neptune's surface, we would see Triton with an apparent width of 37 minutes of arc, or just a little wider than the moon appears to us. The total area of Triton as seen from Neptune is 1.42 times the area of the moon as seen from Earth. Because of the feeble light of the distant sun, however, Triton is only illuminated to about $\frac{1}{150}$ of the brilliance of our own moon, even if we allow for the fact that it is possibly icy and reflects more of the light that falls upon it than the moon does.

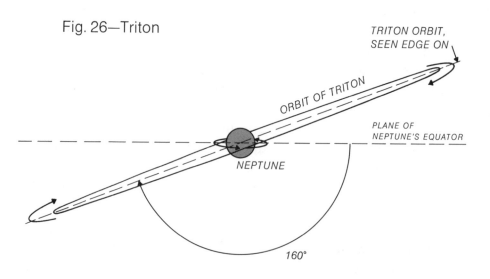

Fig. 26—Triton

Triton is the only satellite in the solar system that appears larger from its planet than the moon does to us.

Triton is also unusually large in comparison with the planet it circles. Triton's mass is 0.0013 times that of Neptune, or about $\frac{1}{750}$. Compare that with Titan, which is only $\frac{1}{4,000}$ as massive as Saturn, or with Ganymede, which is $\frac{1}{12,500}$ as massive as Jupiter. In this respect, however, Triton must still take second place to our moon, which is $\frac{1}{81}$ as massive as Earth.

From Triton, Neptune shines in the sky with a width of just 8 degrees. Neptune then has an area of 235 times that of the moon as it appears to us. Despite this, and despite the fact that Neptune may reflect half the light that falls on it, so little light does fall on it from the pinpoint sun that when Triton sees Neptune in its full phase, it receives only half as much light from its large globe as we received from our much smaller moon.

## Nereid

For a century after the discovery of Neptune, it seemed that Triton, like our moon, was an only satellite. To be sure, at Neptune's great distance it was difficult to see anything but a large satellite and there was a chance that there were a number of small objects circling Neptune that were simply too dim for us to see.

In 1949, Kuiper (who had discovered Miranda, the innermost satellite of Uranus, the year before) detected a small object in Neptune's neighborhood that had a magnitude of only 19. Close observation showed that it was circling Neptune and was, indeed, a second satellite. Kuiper named it Nereid (NEER-ee-id). A nereid is any one of a group of female nymphs who attended Poseidon (Neptune) in the Greek myths. Like Titan, Nereid honors a group of individuals in the myths, rather than a single character.

Nereid has a diameter of about 240 kilometers (150 miles) and its orbit is tipped by 28 degrees to the plane of Neptune's equator. It revolves about Neptune in direct fashion, yet its orbit is by no means a usual one. Nereid's orbit has an eccentricity of 0.75. Of all the satellites in the solar system, Nereid has the most eccentric orbit.

The average distance of Nereid from Neptune is 5,562,000 kilometers (3,456,000 miles). At one end of its elongated orbit, however, Nereid comes within 1,390,000 kilometers (864,000 miles) of Neptune. At the other end, it swoops far out into space and is at a distance of 9,734,000 kilometers (6,050,000 miles) from Neptune, seven times as far away (see Figure 27).

To complete a turn about Neptune, as it travels through this vast ellipse, Nereid takes 359.88 days, or 0.985 years. At its

Fig. 27—Nereid

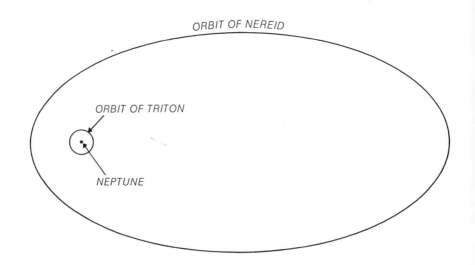

ORBIT OF NEREID

ORBIT OF TRITON

NEPTUNE

greatest distance from Neptune, Nereid moves at an orbital speed of only 0.84 kilometers per second (0.52 miles per second). This is only ⅘ of the orbital speed of our moon. Nereid is the only known satellite in the solar system that ever moves at an orbital speed that is slower than that of our moon.

From Neptune, Nereid would appear in the sky as nothing more than a star; not an extraordinarily bright one, either. At its closest approach it would be one of the brighter second-magnitude stars, about as bright as the North Star. It would then fade from view as it receded farther and farther until, at its farthest point, it would be of the sixth magnitude and just at the borders of visibility to someone with sharp eyes.

From Nereid, Neptune itself changes size dramatically in the course of the satellite's year-long revolution. When Nereid is at its closest to Neptune, the planet would hang in its sky with a diameter of 2 degrees, and with an apparent area some fifteen times that of our moon; but with a total radiance in the dim sunlight of only about ⅛ of our moon.

Then Neptune's globe would shrink slowly from day to day until, half a year later, when Nereid is at its farthest point, Neptune would be only 0.3 degrees across, with an area ⅓ that of the moon and a brightness only 1/350 of it.

Nereid, like Phoebe and the small satellites of Mars and Jupiter, would appear to be a captured asteroid. Its small size, its very elongated orbit, and its considerable orbital inclination all point to this.

Yet if Nereid is a captured asteroid, how did one come to be far out there in the neighborhood of Neptune? That fact that it was seems to favor the notion that the outer reaches of the solar system may contain a large number of asteroids which remain invisible to us only because of their distance.

Of those asteroids, Phoebe was the first discovered, Nereid the second, and Chiron the third. Chiron is the only one of the three, so far, that is not a satellite.

It is not surprising that Phoebe and Nereid were discovered before Chiron was, since the neighborhood of a planet is bound to be more closely studied than blank space is. If we could study every portion of the zodiac as carefully as we study the neighborhood of the planets, we might discover dozens of Chirons.

# 9

## PLUTO

### *The Discovery of Pluto*

Once Uranus had been discovered beyond Saturn, and Neptune beyond Uranus, astronomers were sure to wonder if that was all. Might there not be another planet beyond Neptune?

If so, it would be very difficult to find. It would be far dimmer than Neptune, move still more slowly, have an even smaller orb, and be smothered by an even greater number of stars as bright as itself or brighter.

There seemed no hope of discovering it, even if it existed, unless one had some idea of where it might be in the first place.

Something like that had worked for Neptune, which had been picked out in the place where it should have been to account for the discrepancies in Uranus's motion.

Were there now discrepancies in Neptune's motion that might hint of a still farther planet?

There was a catch here. The farther a planet is from the sun, the longer it takes to complete one revolution. The precision with which astronomers can detect imperfections in the orbital movement depends upon the fraction of the turn the planet has completed.

Thus, Uranus circles the sun in eighty-four years, and in 1846, when Neptune was discovered, Uranus had been under continuous observation for sixty-five years or for 0.77 of its revolutionary period. In addition, there had been a number of observations of Uranus before its actual discovery.

Neptune, however, circles the sun in 165 years, and by 1900 it had been under continuous observation for only fifty-three years and had completed only 0.32 of its revolution. As the twentieth century opened, therefore, Neptune's orbit was not yet known with sufficient precision for it to be very helpful in locating a still more distant planet.

Then what about Uranus? By 1900 it had been continually observed for 1.4 of its revolutions. Once Neptune's pull was taken into account, something like 98 percent of the discrepancy in its orbit was taken care of, but there still remained 2 percent that was not.

Some astronomers tried to use this small residual discrepancy as a guide, even though it was really too small to give very reliable results. The two most careful calculations were those of the American astronomers Percival Lowell (1855–1916) and William Henry Pickering (1858–1938).

Lowell, in his calculations, ended up with a beyond-Neptune planet that seemed to have an orbit that was quite tilted and elliptical. He estimated that its distance from the sun would vary from 5,100,000,000 kilometers (3,200,000,000 miles) at perihelion to 7,700,000,000 kilometers (4,400,000,000 miles) at aphelion. Pickering, on the other hand, calculated the existence of a planet with an orbit less tilted or elliptical, but one that was distinctly more distant from the sun than Lowell's supposed planet was.

Given the orbits, each man could predict the approximate position of his own supposed trans-Neptunian planet at some particular time. In theory one needed only to comb the sky in the indicated area and come up with some star that shouldn't be there according to the star maps, but that wasn't as easy as it sounds.

Neptune was of the eighth magnitude and there were only a reasonable number of stars of eighth magnitude or better and they could all be checked, one by one, in a reasonable time. A more distant planet would be dimmer and would have to be selected out of greater crowds of stars. To be sure, the astronomers of 1900 had photography with which to record a field of stars permanently, something the astronomers of 1846 had not had, but even so the job would prove tedious and difficult.

Pickering, having made his prediction, didn't try very hard to check it out, but Lowell threw himself into the task with consuming eagerness. He worked at Lowell Observatory, which he had built in the clear desert air of Flagstaff, Arizona. His procedure was to take a photograph of a portion of the sky in the region where he thought the planet might be, then another photograph of the same region three days later. In three days, even the slow motion of a trans-Neptunian planet would produce a noticeable shift in position.

After taking the pairs of pictures, Lowell would compare the many stars of one to the many of the other, in a slow and painstaking effort to see if one had changed its position. He did this over and over again for something like eleven years, bending over his plates endlessly, poring over them through a magnifying glass, studying the tiny dots and comparing them.

Again and again he would find a shift, but each time the shift was too great and turned out to represent an asteroid. When he had to be away from the lab, his assistants carried on the search while he wrote to them frequently for news and went over all their plates when he returned, double-checking.

He wore himself out, losing weight and peace of mind, and died of a stroke on November 12, 1916, at the comparatively young age of sixty-one. He had found no new planet.

After Lowell's death, the American astronomer Milton La Salle Humason (1891–1972) took up the search. He used Pickering's figures, and he didn't succeed either.

The next astronomer to take up the task was another American, Clyde William Tombaugh (TOM-boh, 1906–      ), who did his work at Lowell Observatory where the search for the trans-Neptunian planet continued.

Beginning in 1929, Tombaugh had the advantage of a new telescope, one that had a very wide field and could photograph sharply all the stars over a considerably larger area of the sky than had been possible before. Using an exposure of one hour, stars down to the seventeenth magnitude could be recorded and the trans-Neptunian planet, if it existed, was sure to be bright enough, and to spare, for detection.

Tombaugh began to take photographs of the star field in the general region where Lowell's calculations had indicated the planet might be. Many thousands of stars were on each plate.

The task would have continued to be a nearly impossible one except for still another technical advance. Tombaugh had "blink comparator," which Lowell had not had.

The blink comparator could project light through one plate taken on a certain day and then through another plate of the same star region taken a few days later, and do so in rapid alternation. The plates were adjusted so that the stars on each were focused on the same spot. The true stars in the field would then all be in precisely the same position relative to each other and would produce precisely the same projection. The rapid alternation would be so fast that the eye would not detect the flashing but would see a steady, unchanging picture.

If, however, there was a planet present, it would have moved between the times the two photographs were taken and the effect of the blink comparator would be that of showing the planet in one position and then in a new position in rapid alternation. The planet would blink rapidly while all about it were motionless dots.

It was now not necessary to compare each one of the many thousands of stars on one plate with every one of the many thousands of stars on the other. It was only necessary to study every part of the plate in order to catch sight of that tiny blinking alternation and to make sure the motion was too small for it to be caused by an asteroid.

By February 1930, Tombaugh was working through the boundary region between Taurus and Gemini. Here the stars were particularly densely strewn and he found himself struggling with single plates that contained as many as 400,000 stars. Just to give himself a rest, he switched to the other end of Gemini where the stars were sparser and where his plates carried only 50,000 of them.

Then, at 4 P.M. of February 18, 1930, he spotted a blink. It was an object with a magnitude of 14.90 and the shift was a small one of 3.5 millimeters (0.12 inches). With that small shift, it had to be a trans-Neptunian planet. He looked for earlier photographs of the region to see if he could spot a "star" that seemed to have been moving steadily. Knowing where to look, he had no trouble finding it and indeed could trace its planet-like path.

The discovery of the trans-Neptunian planet was formally announced on March 13, 1930, which was the 149th anniversary of the discovery of Uranus and the seventy-fifth anniversary of the birth of Percival Lowell.

There were some suggestions that the new planet be named "Lowell," but that was not seriously considered. A mythological name was needed and Pluto was adopted for the purpose.

It was an appropriate name, for the new planet, farther from the sun than any other, was far enough out into the darkness of space to be named for the mythical god of the dark underworld. In addition, the first two letters of the name were the initials of Percival Lowell.

After the discovery was announced, Humason looked through the plates he had taken some years earlier of the same region of the sky to see if any had contained Pluto. It turned out that two of his plates had Pluto on them, but in both cases it could not be seen. One time a nearby star, brighter than the planet, had drowned it out. The second time its image had just happened to fall on a tiny flaw in the plate.

### The Orbit of Pluto

There were surprises. Pluto was not the planet that either Lowell or Pickering had looked for, since its orbit turned out to be considerably different from the orbit either had calculated. That Pluto had happened to be in a place near where the calculations had shown it would be seemed to be coincidence more than anything else. It just happened to be in a part of its real orbit that skimmed the calculated orbit of Lowell. If it had been in almost any other part of its orbit, it would have been far enough away from the calculated orbit to be found nowhere in the vicinity that Tombaugh would have been looking through.

For one thing, Pluto was not as distant as either Pickering or Lowell had thought it would be. Pickering had felt its average distance from the sun would be 7,800,000,000 kilometers (4,800,000,000 miles) and that it would have a period of revolution of 373 years. Lowell had thought the average distance would be only 6,400,000,000 kilometers (4,000,000,000 miles) and that it would have a period of revolution of 282 years.

In actual fact, Pluto's average distance from the sun turned out to be only 5,900,000,000 kilometers (3,670,000,000 miles) and its period of revolution only 247.7 years.

Even so, Pluto is the farthest planet yet discovered. Its average distance from the sun is nearly one third greater than that of Neptune, and over four times as great as Saturn which, only a century and a half before the discovery of Pluto, had been thought to represent the limit of the visible solar system.

Pluto's period of revolution is 1.5 times as long as that of Neptune and 8.4 times that of Saturn.

There were other surprises. It turned out that the plane of Pluto's orbit is inclined to the ecliptic by 17.2 degrees, which is by far the greatest inclination for any planet. (Until then, the record had been held by Mercury which has an inclination of 7.0 degrees.) Furthermore, the eccentricity of Pluto's orbit is also a planetary record, for it is 0.250. (Again, the previous record had been Mercury's with 0.2056.)

Because of this eccentricity, Pluto at perihelion is only 4,400,000,000 kilometers (2,700,000,000 miles) from the sun. At the opposite end of its orbit, at aphelion, it is 7,400,000,000 kilometers (4,600,000,000 miles) from the sun.

In the neighborhood of perihelion, Pluto actually approaches the sun more closely than Neptune ever does, and is about 100,000,000 kilometers (60,000,000) miles closer to the sun than Neptune is. The result is that when one draws a diagram of the outer solar system as viewed from above (see Figure 28), the orbit of Pluto seems to cross that of Neptune at one end.

This does not mean, however, that Neptune and Pluto can ever crash into each other when both approach the intersection point at the same time. There isn't any actual intersection. The inclination of Pluto's orbit is such that where the two orbits seem to cross, one planet is far above the other (see Figure 29).

Where the two orbits cross, they are separated by a distance of 1,400,000,000 kilometers (870,000,000 miles). What's more, the actual motions of Neptune and Pluto are such that they are never at the "intersection" point or even near it at the same time. The actual closest distance between the planets is about 2,500,000,000 kilometers (1,550,000,000 miles). In fact, Pluto can get closer to Uranus than it ever gets to Neptune. Pluto can approach as closely as 1,600,000,000 kilometers (1,000,000,000 miles) to Uranus.

Fig. 28—The Orbit of Pluto

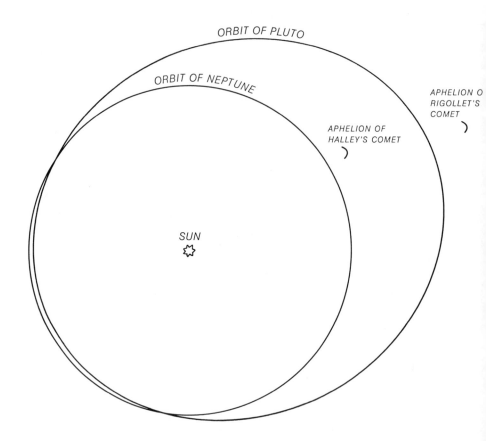

For a period of some twenty years, then, in the neighborhood of its perihelion, Pluto will remain closer to the sun
than Neptune will be, so that Neptune remains the farthest
planet in actuality for about 10 percent of the time. Pluto
will be at perihelion in 1989, so that for the rest of the twentieth century it will see the sun shining just as brightly as
Neptune will.

Fig. 29—Neptune and Pluto

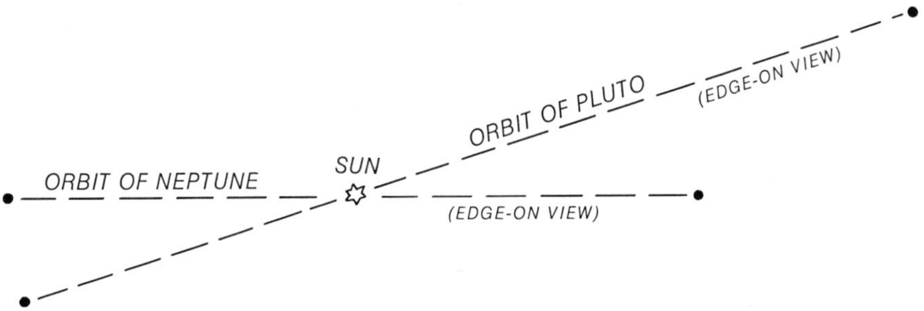

But then it will be moving out to aphelion, which it will reach next in 2113. To Pluto at aphelion, the sun is only $\frac{1}{2450}$ as bright as it is to us on Earth. Even then, the sun sheds 190 times the amount of light upon Pluto that the full moon delivers to Earth.

Halley's comet, at aphelion, reaches a distance of only 5,240,000,000 kilometers (3,250,000,000 miles) from the sun. This is well beyond Neptune's orbit and is beyond Pluto's distance at its perihelion. However, the aphelion distance of Halley's comet is only seven tenths as far as the aphelion distance of Pluto.

Rigollet's comet, the one with the longest determined orbit, is, at aphelion, 8,500,000,000 kilometers (5,300,000,000 miles) from the sun, and this is 1.15 times as far as Pluto ever gets. At aphelion, an observer on Rigollet's comet would see the sun with a brightness equal to only 140 times that of our full moon.

Other comets whose orbits have not been precisely determined undoubtedly recede to farther distances still, and uncounted numbers may be at vast distances at all times so that we never see them. Any comet at a distance of 100,000,000,000 kilometers (62,000,000,000 miles) from the sun—twelve times the aphelion distance of Rigollet's comet—would see the sun deliver no more light than the full moon does to us, and at greater distances it would deliver still less. To the very farthest comets, it may well be that the sun appears as no more than a bright star, only slightly brighter than Sirius at most.

## The Size of Pluto

A disturbing suspicion concerning Pluto arose at once when its magnitude, at the time of discovery, was found to be 14.90. That was too low. If Neptune were at the position of even Pluto's aphelion, its magnitude would still be about 10. For Pluto to be so dim must mean, then, that it was considerably smaller than Neptune.

At first it was thought that Pluto might be at least the size of Earth, but in 1950 Kuiper managed to get a view of Pluto as a tiny disc and, measuring its apparent size, calculated its diameter as 5,800 kilometers (3,600 miles). This is less than the diameter of Mars.

Astronomers were reluctant to believe it and some thought up ways in which Kuiper might have been mistaken. However, on April 28, 1965, Pluto passed very close to a faint star, and all doubts ceased. The center of Pluto was passing so close to the star that if its diameter had been greater than that of Mars, Pluto's edge would have moved in front of the star and blacked it out. The star remained shining, however, so Pluto was definitely smaller than Mars.

If anything, in fact, its size may be smaller still. In 1976, analysis of light reflected from it made it appear to have a surface that is covered with frozen methane. But when an object like Pluto forms, it grows hot in the process and if it were the size of Earth, or even of Mars, it would have grown hot enough to vaporize the methane and its small gravity would then not have been able to hold it. The smaller a body is, the less it heats up on forming, and to retain the methane, Pluto would have to be rather smaller than our moon—satellite-size, in short, and not planet-size. Right now, Pluto's surface temperature may attain a height of —233° C. (—388° F.) or only 40 degrees C. over obsolute zero.

Clearly, an object the size of Pluto, which never approaches more closely to Uranus than 1,600,000,000 kilometers (1,000,-000,000 miles), couldn't possibly account for the small discrepancies that remain in Uranus's orbit. Whatever Pluto is, it is not the planet whose presence was calculated from those discrepancies by Lowell and by Pickering.

Does that mean there is a "real" trans-Neptunian planet that still exists out there and that *is* the cause of the orbital discrepancies that remain in Uranus's motion? If so, it is probably more distant than Pluto and probably considerably more massive.

Despite its greater distance, such a trans-Neptunian planet would be brighter than Pluto and would show a larger orb, but it would be moving more slowly than Pluto and that would make it harder to detect. For the very distant planets, it is motion rather than brightness or appearance that gives them away.

In 1955 it was noticed that Pluto's magnitude varied slightly in a regular way. The period of variation is 6.3874 days, and there is a general feeling that this represents its period of rotation. The surface may be unevenly covered with methane so that the brightness goes up as the icier hemisphere comes into view and then goes down as the rockier one appears.

This is an unexpectedly slow period of rotation. To be sure, it is not as slow as that of Mercury and Venus, but the latter two bodies are close to the sun and tidal effects undoubtedly slowed their rotation. What tidal effect could have slowed Pluto's rotation?

The English astronomer Raymond Arthur Lyttleton suggested that the culprit may have been Neptune. Could it be that Pluto, no larger than Triton, was once a satellite of Neptune, like Triton, and that Neptune's tidal effects had slowed Pluto's rotation until it faced one side always to Neptune? In that case, its period of rotation would be equal to its period of revolution about Neptune.

If so, however, Neptune might have been very unusual in having two large satellites at almost equal distances. Triton, at a distance of 355,000 kilometers (220,000 miles), circles Neptune in 5.88 days. For Pluto to circle Neptune in 6.39 days, it would have to be at a distance of 375,000 kilometers (233,000 miles).

To have two large satellites in close proximity might have set the stage for some instability. Something happened that sent Pluto careening wildly outward into its present orbit, while Triton's orbit was tipped so far around as to cause it to continue its revolution in a retrograde manner.

This suggestion, although interesting, gives rise to numerous difficulties. What exactly caused the catastrophe? How could it send Pluto into an orbit that kept it so far removed from Neptune at all times? How could Triton's orbit be so tampered with and yet remain almost perfectly circular?

And then, on June 22, 1978, there came a discovery that seemed to explain everything. On that day, the American astronomer James W. Christy, examining photographs of Pluto, noticed a distinct bump on one side. He examined other photographs and finally decided that Pluto had a satellite. It was quite close to Pluto, not more than 20,000 kilometers (12,500 miles) away, center to center. At the distance of Pluto, that's not much of a separation, which accounts for the long-delayed discovery.

Christy named the satellite Charon, after the ferryman who took shades across the River Styx to Hades. (It is a poor name, since Chiron had been discovered not long before and the two names are bound to be confused.)

Charon circles Pluto in 6.39 days, which is just the time it takes for Pluto to turn on its axis. This is not a coincidence. It must be that the two bodies, Pluto and Charon, have slowed each other by tidal action until each always faces the same side to the other. They now revolve about a common center of gravity like the two halves of a dumbbell held together by a gravitational pull.

From the distance of separation and the time of revolution, it is possible to work out the total mass of both bodies; it turns out to be only about ⅛ the mass of the moon. Pluto is far smaller than anyone had thought. In fact, Pluto seems to be about 3000 kilometers (1850 miles) in diameter and Charon about 1200 kilometers (750 miles) in diameter.

Charon may have as much as 10 percent the mass of Pluto, which makes the two bodies virtually a double planet—much more so than are the Earth and the moon, since the moon is only about 1.2 percent the mass of the Earth.

It is hard to think of Pluto as a planet now. Perhaps it is one more of the Chiron-like bodies that may fill the outer solar system. If so, we now know five of them: Chiron itself, Phoebe, Nereid, Pluto, and Charon.

The recent discoveries of Uranus's rings, of Chiron and of Charon should convince us that there are surprises far out there and probably much more will be discovered. Certainly, there are puzzles that remain.

How large are the particles of Saturn's rings, for instance, and of what are they composed?

What is the surface of Titan like, considering that it is the only satellite known to have an atmosphere?

Why does Uranus rotate on its side?

Why do Phoebe and Nereid have such unusual orbits?

Are there additional objects like Chiron in the outer solar system?

Why is Triton revolving in retrograde fashion?

What are Uranus's rings like in detail and does Neptune have rings, too?

What more can we find out about Pluto and Charon?

Whatever the probes tell us, the results are bound to delight and astonish us.

# GLOSSARY

ALBEDO—The fraction of sunlight reflected by a planet or satellite.

AMMONIA—A substance with molecules made up of a nitrogen atom and three hydrogen atoms ($NH_3$).

ANGLE—A figure formed when two straight lines meet at a point or when two planes meet along a line.

APHELION—The point in a planet's orbit where it is farthest from the sun.

AREA—The extent of the surface of any object.

ARGON—A gas making up $\frac{1}{100}$ of the Earth's atmosphere.

ASTEROID—A small planet.

ASTEROID BELT—The region between the orbits of Mars and Jupiter where most of the asteroids are to be found.

ASTRONOMICAL UNIT—The average distance of the Earth from the sun.

ATMOSPHERE—The layer of gases surrounding a planet, satellite, or star.

AXIAL TIP—The angle between the axis of rotation of an object and a line perpendicular to its plane of revolution.

AXIS OF ROTATION—The imaginary straight line about which an object spins.

BASE LINE—The distance between two observation points in determining parallax.

BLINK COMPARATOR—A device for projecting two photos of the same region of the sky in rapid alternation to see whether one object shifts its position.

CARBON—A black solid; one of the common elements of the universe.

CARBON DIOXIDE—A gas found in Earth's atmosphere in small quantities; found in the atmospheres of Mars and Venus in large quantities.

CENTIMETER—A measure of length, equal to about ⅖ of an inch.

CENTRIFUGAL EFFECT—The tendency for anything spinning about a center to move away from that center.

CIRCUMFERENCE—The total length of the curve of a circle or similar shape; the length of a curve marked around the widest part of a sphere or similar shape.

COMA—A haze of dust and gas surrounding the central region of a comet.

COMET—An object moving about the sun in an eccentric orbit and composed of materials some of which, on warming up near the sun, drift away from the comet to form a "tail."

COMETOID—A comet that is far enough from the sun so that all its substance is hard solid.

CUBIC METER—A cube one meter on each side; equal to 35.3 cubic feet.

DEGREE—An angular measure equal to $\frac{1}{360}$ the circumference of a circle.

DENSITY—The mass of an object divided by its volume.

DIAMETER—The length of a line passing across the widest part of a circle or sphere and through the center of the circle or sphere.

DIRECT MOTION—Turning motion in the same direction as Earth's rotation; the common direction of turning in the solar system.

ECCENTRICITY—Degree to which the ellipse of an elliptical orbit is flattened.

ECLIPSE—The covering from view of an object in the sky by another object that moves in front of it.

ECLIPTIC—The plane that passes through the center of the sun and through all points of Earth's orbit.

ELEMENT—One of the simple substances making up the universe.

ELLIPSE—A curve that looks like a flattened circle.

ELLIPSOID—A solid that looks like a flattened sphere.

EQUATOR—The circumference that lies halfway between the two poles of a spinning object.

EQUATORIAL BULGE—The extra thickness of a planet in the equatorial regions due to the centrifugal effect of its rotation.

EQUATORIAL DIAMETER—The diameter stretching from a point on the equator to the opposite point on the equator.

ESCAPE VELOCITY—The speed with which an object must move to escape from the gravitational pull of a planet, satellite, or star.

ETHANE—A substance with a molecule made up of two carbon atoms and six hydrogen atoms ($C_2H_6$).

ETHYLENE—A substance with a molecule made up of two carbon atoms and four hydrogen atoms ($C_2H_4$).

FOCUS (plural, foci)—One of two points inside an ellipse. The two foci are at equal distances from the center of the ellipse and on opposite sides, along the major axis.

GALILEAN SATELLITES—The four large satellites of Jupiter; so called because they were discovered by Galileo.

GAS—A form of matter in which atoms and molecules are widely spread out and move freely; air is the most common example.

GAS GIANTS—The giant planets—Jupiter, Saturn, Uranus, and Neptune; so called because they consist largely of substances which are gases on Earth.

GRAM—A measure of weight equal to about $\frac{1}{27}$ of an ounce.

GRAVITATION—The attraction exerted by one object on the other objects in the universe.

HELIUM—A gas composed of the second simplest of all atoms.

HYDROCARBON—A substance whose molecules are made up entirely of carbon and hydrogen atoms.

HYDROGEN—A gas composed of the simplest of all atoms.

HYDROGEN SULFIDE—A substance with molecules made up of two hydrogen atoms and a sulfur atom ($H_2S$).

ICES—Substances which are liquids or gases on Earth and which freeze into brittle, white solids resembling ordinary water ice in appearance.

INCLINATION—The angle between the plane of the orbit of a planet and the ecliptic.

INNER SOLAR SYSTEM—That portion of the solar system stretching outward to the orbit of Mars.

IRON—A gray metal; the most common of the metals in the universe.

KILOGRAM—A measure of mass equal to 1000 grams, or about 2.2 pounds.

KILOMETER—A measure of length equal to about ⅝ of a mile.

LONG-PERIOD COMETS—Those comets which move far beyond the planets at aphelion and which do not return to the inner solar system oftener than once in hundreds of thousands of years, or which remain far away at all times.

MAGNESIUM—One of the common metals making up the universe.

MAGNETIC FIELD—A region in which electromagnetic forces make themselves felt.

MAGNITUDE—A figure representing the apparent brightness of an object shining in the sky. The lower the figure, the brighter the object.

MAJOR AXIS—A diameter passing through the foci and center of an ellipse.

MASS—In a general way, the amount of matter in an object.

METHANE—A substance with molecules made up of a carbon atom and four hydrogen atoms ($CH_4$).

MINOR AXIS—A diameter of an ellipse that is at right angles to the major axis.

MINUTE OF ARC—An angular measure equal to ¹⁄₆₀ of a degree.

MOLECULE—A group of atoms held together by electromagnetic forces.

NEON—A gas like helium but made up of more complicated atoms.

NITROGEN—A gas making up ⅘ of the Earth's atmosphere.

NODE—The point at which a planet's orbit crosses the ecliptic.

OBLATENESS—The flattening of a planet from spherical form because of the centrifugal force of rotation.

ORBIT—The path taken by an object revolving about a larger object.

ORBITAL SPEED—The speed with which an object moves in its orbit.

OUTER PLANETS—The planets whose orbits are beyond that of Mars.

OXYGEN—An active gas making up ⅕ of the Earth's atmosphere.

PARABOLA—A curve like an ellipse that has stretched so far that it never closes again.

PARALLAX—The apparent change of position of a close object compared to a more distant object, when the viewer shifts the position from which he views the object.

PERIHELION—The point in a planet's orbit where it is closest to the sun.

PERIOD OF REVOLUTION—The time it takes an object to make one complete turn about a larger object.

PERIOD OF ROTATION—The time it takes an object to spin once on its axis.

PLANE—A geometric figure that is perfectly flat and without thickness.

PLANET—Originally, an object in the sky which moved against the background of the stars. Now it is used for any object that circles a star and shines only by reflected light.

POLAR DIAMETER—The diameter stretching from north pole to south pole.

POLES—The points where the axis of rotation reaches the surface of the rotating body.

RADIATION—Energy or particles which move outward from some source in all directions.

RADIUS—The distance from the center to the surface; half the distance of the diameter.

RETROGRADE MOTION—Motion in a direction opposite to what is usual.

REVOLUTION—The circling of an object about another object.

ROCHE LIMIT—The distance from an object's center within which tidal effect will disrupt a neighboring and smaller object.

ROTATION—The spinning of an object about its own central axis.

SATELLITE—An object that revolves about a planet.

SECOND OF ARC—An angular measure equal to $\frac{1}{60}$ of a minute of arc.

SILICATES—Substances made up of molecules containing silicon and oxygen atoms; almost all rocks are silicates.

SILICON—A semimetallic element that is a common constituent of the universe.

SOLAR SYSTEM—The sun and all the objects that are held in its gravitational field and that move around it.

SOLAR WIND—Charged particles from the sun moving out at high velocity in every direction.

STAR—One of the objects visible in the sky as a tiny spark of light.

SULFUR—A solid, yellow substance.

SURFACE—The outside of any solid object.

SURFACE GRAVITY—The strength of the gravitational pull on the surface of a planet or satellite.

TELESCOPE—A tube, containing lenses or mirrors, which makes distant objects look larger, nearer, and brighter.

TIDAL EFFECT—The manner in which the gravitation of one body affects different parts of another body differently, thus distorting the second body.

TITIUS-BODE LAW—A set of numbers representing the distances from the sun of the planets of the solar system.

TROJAN ASTEROIDS—Asteroids traveling in Jupiter's orbit, but either 60° ahead or 60° behind Jupiter.

VOLUME—The room taken up by any object.

WATER—A substance with molecules made up of two hydrogen atoms and an oxygen atom ($H_2O$).

WAVELENGTH—The length of a wave of light and of radiations similar to light.

# INDEX

Achilles, 142, 143
Adams, John Couch, 177
Airy, George Biddell, 177
albedo, 49
Amalthea, 119
angle, 35, 36
aphelion, 26
Ariel, 163
Aristotle, 133
asteroid belt, 141
asteroids, 140, 141
Astronomical Unit, 24, 29
atmosphere, 97, 98
    Jupiter's, 84, 85
    Saturn's, 85
axis, 51

Baade, Walter, 141, 145
Barnard, Edward Emerson, 103
blink comparator, 198
Bode, Johann Elert, 153, 176
Bond, William Cranch, 64, 102
Borelli, Giovanni Alfonso, 134
Bouvard, Alexis, 173

Canopus, 154, 155
Cassini, Giovanni Domenico, 29, 64,
    101, 102
Cassini's Division, 64, 68, 128–130
centimeter, 38
centrifugal effect, 51

Ceres, 140
    Titius-Bode law and, 176
Challis, James, 177
Charon, 206, 207
Chiron, 147, 148, 193, 194, 207
    orbit, 148–150
    Uranus and, 157
Christy, James W., 206
cometoids, 138
comets, 133ff.
    far-distant, 137, 138
    orbits, 135
    parallax, 134
    structure, 137
    tail, 134, 137
Copernicus, Nicolaus, 17

D'Arrest, Heinrich Ludwig, 178
degree, 35
density, 77
Dione, 102
    structure, 131
direct motion, 114
Dollfus, Audoin, 104

Earth, 28
    atmosphere, 98
    axial tipping, 58
    brightness, 45
    density, 78
    distance from sun, 29
    equatorial bulge, 54

moon's pull on, 68, 69
rotation, 52, 69
eccentricity, 22
ecliptic, 35
elements, 80, 81
Elliot, James L., 170
ellipse, 21–23
ellipsoid, 52
Enceladus, 102
Encke, Johann Franz, 135, 178
Encke's comet, 135, 137
equatorial bulge, 52
Eros, 141
escape velocity, 88

Flamsteed, John, 157
Fracastoro, Girolamo, 134
foci, 22, 23

Galilean satellites, 75, 88ff., 95
Galileo, 29, 59, 60, 75
Galle, Johann Gottfried, 178
gas giants, 84
gases, 81
Gauss, Johann K. F., 140
George III, 153
gravitation, 33

Halley, Edmund, 135
Halley's comet, 135–137, 203
Herschel, John, 75, 101
Herschel, William, 53, 102, 152, 153, 162
Hidalgo, 145, 146
Hipparchus, 43
Humason, Milton La Salle, 197, 199
Huygens, Christian, 61–64, 68, 75, 101
hydrocarbons, 99
Hyperion, 102
Titan seen from, 121, 122

Iapetus, 101, 102
brightness, 131, 132
diameter, 124–126
Saturn's rings seen from, 122, 123
Icarus, 141, 142
ices, 81
inner solar system, 31
iron, 82

Janus, 104
Cassini's Division and, 129, 130
orbit, 110, 111
Saturn as seen from, 118, 119
Jupiter, 17
atmosphere, 84, 85
brightness, 45
magnetic field, 123, 124
mass, 77, 189
satellites, 75, 103, 106, 110, 111
telescopic appearance, 50, 51
Uranus and, 173
volume, 47

Kepler, Johannes, 21, 60, 75
kilometer, 28n
Kohoutek, Lubos, 139
Kohoutek's comet, 139
Kowall, Charles, 147
Kuiper, Gerard Peter, 99, 163, 191, 204

Lagrange, Joseph Louis, 143
Lalande, Joseph Jérôme de, 179
Laplace, Pierre Simon de, 70
Lassell, William, 163, 186
lead, 21
Lemonnier, Pierre Charles, 157
Leverrier, Urbain J. J., 178
Lexell, Anders Jean, 153
light, 84
velocity, 30
Lowell, Percival, 196, 197
Lyttleton, Raymond Arthur, 206

magnitudes, 43
major axis, 22, 23
Mars, 17
brightness, 45
parallax, 29
Maxwell, James Clerk, 71
Mercury, 16
size, 91
sun's radiation and, 42
width of sun as seen from, 40, 41
metals, 82
methane, 99, 166, 204, 205
Mimas, 102
Cassini's Division and, 129, 130
minor axis, 22, 23

minutes of arc, 39
Miranda, 163
moon, 16
    brightness, 44n
    distance, 28
    pull on Earth, 68, 69
    rotation, 69
    telescopic appearance, 50
    tidal breakup, 71, 72

Neptune, 177–179
    apparent motion, 182
    as seen from Nereid, 193
    as seen from Triton, 191
    axial tilt, 183, 185
    brightness, 182
    density, 188
    diameter, 183
    early sightings, 179
    equatorial speed, 185
    escape velocity, 188
    mass, 187
    name, 179
    oblateness, 185
    orbit, 180, 181
    orbital eccentricity, 180
    orbital inclination, 180
    orbital speed, 182
    period of revolution, 182
    period of rotation, 183, 185
    Pluto and, 201–203, 206
    sun seen from, 185
    surface gravity, 188, 189
    Titius-Bode law and, 180
Nereid, 191
  as seen from Neptune, 193
    diameter, 192
    orbit, 192
    orbital speed, 193
    period of revolution, 192
Newton, Isaac, 33, 51
nodes, 37

Oberon, 162
oblateness, 55, 56
Oort, Jan Hendrik, 137
orbit, 21
orbital inclination 114–116

parabola, 134
parallax, 27

Parker, Eugene Newman, 137
Patroclus, 143
perihelion, 24, 26
Phobos, 119
Phoebe, 103, 150
    orbit, 106, 109
    orbital eccentricity, 112, 113
    orbital inclination, 116–118
    Saturn's rings seen from, 123
Piazzi, Giuseppe, 140
Pickering, William Henry, 103, 196, 197
Pioneer 10 and 11, 85, 93
plane, 34
planets, 17
    albedo, 49
    aphelia, 26, 27
    apparent width, 46
    atmosphere, 98
    axial tipping, 56–58
    axis, 56
    brightness, 44, 45
    days of the week and, 21
    density, 78, 79
    diameter, 46, 47
    distance from sun, 30
    distance from the ecliptic, 37
    equator, 56
    equatorial speed, 54
    escape velocity from, 87, 88
    formation, 83, 84
    inclination to the ecliptic, 35, 36
    mass, 76, 77
    metals and, 20, 21
    names, 19, 20
    oblateness, 55, 56
    orbital eccentricity, 24, 25
    orbital velocity, 34
    perihelia, 26, 27
    period of revolution, 17, 18
    period of rotation, 53
    polar diameter, 54, 55
    radiation received from sun, 41, 42
    relative distance, 18, 19
    relative distance from sun, 24, 25
    relative size, 47, 48
    revolution, 57
    Roche limit, 72, 73
    satellites, 101–104

surface gravity, 85–87
telescopic appearance. 50, 51
width of sun as seen from, 40–41
planets, outer, 180
   density, 188
   diameter, 183
   distance from sun, 180
   equatorial speed, 185
   escape velocity from. 188
   mass, 187
   oblateness, 185
   orbital speed, 182
   orbits, 182
   period of revolution, 182
   period of rotation, 185
   relative size, 184
   surface gravity, 188
Pluto, 196–199
   aphelion, 201
   as double planet, 207
   brightness, 204
   diameter, 204, 207
   distance from sun, 200
   mass, 207
   name, 199
   Neptune and, 201–203. 206
   orbit, 201, 202
   orbital eccentricity, 201
   orbital inclination, 201
   perihelion, 201, 202
   period of revolution. 200
   period of rotation, 205
   satellite, 206, 207
   sun as seen from, 202. 203
   temperature, 205
   Uranus and, 201

Regiomontanus, 134
retrograde motion, 114
Rhea, 102
Richer, Jean, 29
Rigollet's comet, 136, 203
rings, Saturn's, 61
   area, 67
   as seen from Saturn's satellites, 122, 123
   disappearance, 62. 63
   origin, 71–73
   period of revolution. 110
   Saturn as seen from. 119, 120

size, 64–66
structure, 70, 71
tidal effects, 70, 71
tipping, 62, 63
volume, 68, 72, 73
rings, Uranus's, 169–172
Roche, Edouard, 71, 72
Roche limit, 72, 73
rocks, 82

satellites, 74, 75
   as seen from planets, 95, 97
   atmosphere, 99
   brightness, 88, 89
   density, 93, 94
   diameter, 90
   escape velocity from, 95, 96
   mass, 93, 94, 186, 187
   Mercury and, 91
   surface gravity, 95, 96
   volume, 90, 91
   volume compared to planets, 92
satellites, Jupiter's, 111, 113, 114, 116, 128, 145
satellites, Mars's, 142
satellites, Neptune's, 186ff.
satellites, Saturn's, 101–105
   as seen from Saturn, 126, 127
   brightness, 124, 125
   density, 131, 132
   diameter, 124–126
   distance from Saturn, 105, 106
   mass, 128, 129
   orbit, 105–109
   orbital eccentricity, 111, 112
   orbital inclination, 115, 116
   period of revolution, 110, 111
   Saturn as seen from, 118, 119
   sun as seen from, 120, 121
   surface gravity, 128, 130
satellites, Pluto's, 206–207
satellites, Uranus's, 162–163
   as seen from Uranus, 167
   brightness, 163
   diameter, 166
   distance from Uranus, 163, 164
   mass, 166
   names, 162, 163
   orbit, 163–165
   period of revolution, 163, 164
Saturday, 21

Saturn, 17
    albedo, 49
    aphelion, 26, 27, 31
    apparent width, 46
    appearance from satellites, 118,
        119
    atmosphere, 84, 85
    axial tipping, 58
    brightness, 44, 45
    density, 78, 79
    diameter, 47
    distance from Earth, 33
    distance from sun, 24, 25, 30
    distance from the ecliptic, 37
    equatorial bulge, 55
    equatorial speed, 54
    escape velocity from, 88
    formation, 83, 84
    Hidalgo and, 146
    inclination to the ecliptic, 35, 36
    lead and, 21
    magnetic field, 124
    mass, 76, 77
    name, 20
    oblateness, 55, 56
    orbital eccentricity, 24, 25
    orbital velocity, 34
    perihelion, 26, 27, 31
    period of revolution, 17, 19
    period of rotation, 53
    polar diameter, 55
    radiation received from sun, 42,
        43
    rings, 61ff.
    Roche limit, 72, 73
    surface area, 47
    surface gravity, 85–87
    telescopic appearance, 50, 51,
        59–61
    Uranus and, 173
    volume, 47
    width of sun as seen from, 40,
        41
Scheiner, Christoph, 60
Schwassman-Wachmann's comet, 139
silicates, 82
Sirius, 44, 154, 155
solar system, 18
    diagram, 32
    general makeup, 82
    origin, 79ff.
    shape, 34, 35
solar wind, 137
stars, 15
    brightness, 43
sun, 15
    apparent size, 39–41
    as seen from comets, 203, 204
    as seen from Saturn's satellites,
        120, 121
    as seen from Neptune, 185
    as seen from Pluto, 202, 203
    as seen from Uranus, 160, 161
    brightness, 44n

tail, comet's, 134
Taylor, Gordon, 169
telescopes, 29
Tethys, 102
tidal effect, 69, 70
Titan, 75
    as seen from Hyperion, 121, 122
    atmosphere, 99
    brightness, 89
    brightness from Saturn, 97
    density, 93, 94
    diameter, 89, 90
    distance from Saturn, 76
    escape velocity from, 95, 96
    mass, 93, 94
    Mercury and, 91
    period of revolution, 76
    size from Saturn, 97
    structure, 95
    surface, 99, 100
    surface gravity, 95, 96
    volume, 91, 126
    volume compared to Saturn, 92
Titania, 162
Titius, Johann Daniel, 175
Titius-Bode law, 175, 176
Tombaugh, Clyde William, 198, 199
Triton, 186
    as seen from Neptune, 190, 191
    brightness, 186
    diameter, 186
    mass, 186, 187, 190
    orbit, 186
    orbital inclination, 189
    size relative to Neptune, 191

Trojan asteroids, 143–145
Tycho Brahe, 134

Umbriel, 163
Uranus, 152–153
    apparent motion, 155, 156
    apparent size, 155, 156
    as seen from satellites, 167–169
    axial tilt, 159, 160
    brightness, 154, 155
    density, 164
    diameter, 159
    distance from sun, 157
    early sightings, 156, 157
    equatorial speed, 185
    escape velocity from, 188
    mass, 164
    motion, 173, 174
    name, 153, 154
    oblateness, 159, 185

    orbit, 157–159
    orbital speed, 182
    period of rotation, 159
    Pluto and, 201
    rings, 169–172
    satellites, 162ff.
    structure, 164, 166
    sun and, 160, 161
    surface gravity, 188, 189
    temperature, 162
    Titius-Bode law and, 175

Venus, 16
    brightness of, 44, 45
Von Struve, Friedrich G. W., 64

Whipple, Fred Lawrence, 137
Wildt, Rupert, 84, 166
Witt, Gustav, 141
Wolf, Max, 142

## About the Author

ISAAC ASIMOV is a versatile and prolific writer. *Saturn and Beyond* is his 199th book. He is a scientist, a science writer, a futurist, one of the great science fiction writers of all time.

Born in Russia, he came to the United States at the age of three and grew up in Brooklyn, New York. At Columbia University he earned the degrees of B.S., M.A., and Ph.D., and for nine years taught biochemistry at the Boston University School of Medicine, where he still holds the title of Associate Professor.

A noted wit and raconteur, he is in great demand as a speaker, and has received countless awards and honors. He and his wife live in a New York City apartment with a telescope and an unobstructed view of the skies.